ETHICS FOR A SMALL PLANET

SUNY Series in Religious Studies
Harold Coward, Editor

ETHICS FOR A SMALL PLANET

New Horizons on Population,
Consumption, and Ecology

DANIEL C. MAGUIRE
AND
LARRY L. RASMUSSEN

With an Introduction by
Rosemary Radford Ruether

State University of New York Press

Permission is acknowledged for the following citations: Alfred W. Crosby, *Ecological Imperialism: The Biological Expansion of Europe, 900–1900*, Cambridge University Press, 1986; Peony from *Upstairs in the Garden: Poems Selected & New, 1968–1988*, Norton, 1990; Larry Rasmussen, *Earth Community, Earth Ethics*, Orbis Books, 1996; William C. Clark, "Managing Planet Earth," *Scientific American*, Vol. 261, September 1989:48; David Korten, "Sustainable Development Strategies: The People-Centered Consensus," a paper from the People-Centered Development Forum, 17 May 1994.

Published by
State University of New York Press, Albany

For information, address State University of New York
Press, State University Plaza, Albany, N.Y. 12246.

Production by E. Moore
Marketing by Hannah J. Hazen

Library of Congress Cataloging-in-Publication Data

Maguire, Daniel C.
    Ethics for a small planet : New horizons on population,
consumption, and ecology / Daniel C. Maguire and Larry L. Rasmussen.
        p.   cm. — (SUNY series in religious studies)
    Includes bibliographical references and index.
    ISBN 0-7914-3645-4 (hardcover : alk. paper). — ISBN 0-7914-3646-2
(pbk. : alk. paper)
        1. Human ecology—Religious aspects—Christianity.
    2. Environmental ethics. 3. Christian ethics. 4. Social ethics.
    I. Rasmussen, Larry L. II. Title. III. Series.
    BT695.5.M34 1997
    241'.691—dc21   97-9361
                                                                           CIP

10 9 8 7 6 5 4 3 2 1

Contents

Preface

The topic of this book is the suffering of this planet and its people. The undergoading theme is on male power, specifically white and Western male power. Of course, male planetary power is changing colors as economies burgeon in the East, where men are once again exercising their traditional and seemingly universal genius for monarchical power, even in countries that are supposedly democratic.

Thrones are a permanent human temptation. You can do a lot on a throne. You can write the script, define reality, determine what and who is sacred; you can have one rule for the "noble" courtiers and one for the commoners, and you can use people as compost for your privileges. Who, at some base level, would not want to be royal!

One modern throne is the *economy* with its structures of privilege and there we find—surprise!—mostly men—like the pharaohs of old, royally and hegemonically perched.

But, another even superior throne is *theory*, whether dressed in theological, philosophical, or social-science garb. Theory is the Acropolis overlooking the city, casting its defining shadows. Theory crafts the scepter. The shape of the scepter changes from age to age, but its persistent core is status. Those who define status—the status of the earth, the status of people—hold and confer the power. Economic and political activists are duly warned to take heed, for they are destined to be the pawns of those who think and theorize. More often than they believe, they are doing the bidding of those who dare to theorize and set the symbols whereby we define ourselves.

Theory is power, and most of Western theological, philosophical, and economic theory has been written by men, royally and hegemonically perched men.

And here is a volume written by two more of them. First, Daniel C. Maguire goes beyond Lynn White by inculpating religions and their Gods for our planetary plight and yet he sees the emergence of a new sense of the sacred that could signal a moral mutation in the evolution of our species. Larry L. Rasmussen, working out of his earlier study *Earth Community, Earth Ethics* (Orbis, 1996) probes the terracidal and genocidal shadows of "progress" and the fatal historic efforts to make the world into a Euro-American civilization writ large.

But have we not heard quite enough from men? No. Why? Because just as feminism is unfinished business until men are feminists, men must look at what they and their fellows tracing back to antiquity have wrought. The voices of the beleaguered and "wretched of the earth" and the wretched earth itself will continue to cry in pain until they— the victim gender and the victim earth—are joined in common quest with those who have too long basked in the sick aura of purloined privilege.

Maleness is wealth in a sexist world, unjust wealth. Until its counterfeit nature is discovered especially by those who have profited from it, until this rapacious elitism is no longer common currency, a revolutionary job waits to be done and the earth will continue to die.

This volume is an offering by two white, comfortable, Western, male theorists.

DANIEL C. MAGUIRE

Acknowledgments

The authors acknowledge the generous support of the Ford Foundation and the John D. and Catherine T. MacArthur Foundations for the Religious Consultation on Population, Reproductive Health and Ethics which sponsored this volume.

INTRODUCTION

ROSEMARY RADFORD RUETHER

These are two wise and helpful essays which focus on the profound challenge to the human enterprise on planet earth posed by burgeoning human population and the gargantuan use of resources by an affluent elite of this population. Both ask the questions of how male domination, as white European domination, has contributed to this problem of earth crisis and whether Christianity can be a part of the solution, rather than just a part of the problem.

Daniel Maguire, social ethicist teaching at Marquette University in Milwaukee, Wisconsin, compares two countries, Egypt and China, venues of two important world conferences, the United Nations Conference on Population and Development in 1994 and the Fourth World Conference on Women in 1995. Egypt represents a disaster area of pollution, burgeoning population, the split between the affluent lifestyle of an elite and the impoverishment of the majority. Once the grain basket of the Mediterranean world, Egypt today feeds most of its grain to livestock for a meat diet affordable only by the wealthy few.

China also represents a land of dense population. More than a fifth of the population of the world, 1.28 billion, lives there in a mountainous country with limited land suitable to feed this population. Its centralized communist government has decided that it must take draconian measures to control this population in order to assure a minimum means of life for all. Its one-child policy has succeeded in 20 years in reducing its fertility rate by a third.

The world consensus that emerged from the conference on population and development is that coercive methods of population control are out and the focus should be women's empowerment and development, with the assumption that if women were fully equal they would voluntarily choose to have fewer children. Maguire applauded this affirmation of women's agency, but challenges the libertarian assumptions that global society can simply leave the population issue up to every individual woman and family. Individual rights need to be balanced by questions of the common good, and there is a proper role of government in setting limits on population and consumption, as they do in other areas, for the sake of the welfare of the community.

Maguire also challenges the notion that commitment to the common good of humanity as a whole on a common earth can be fired only by statistics and rational analysis. There needs to be a revival of the sense of the sacred, of awe and reverence for the presence of the divine in and through the whole earth house. There is a great thirst for such a renewed sense of the sacred among people today, but the Christian churches are not able to nourish it. Christians, most prominently among them, women, are departing from the churches, not out of secular disenchantment, but in search of a new experience of the enchantment of the natural world.

The old patterns of Christianity that fostered the separation of a male-dominating God from nature, an exclusivist Christology and a focus on heaven, not earth, as our true home, are dying, and deservedly so, for they have been major causes of a loss of a holistic sense of the sacred in and through life here on earth. There is a need to find a new common ground between religions based on the sense of the sacred that links us all together and which can inspire commitment to the common good of the earth.

Larry L. Rasmussen, social ethicist teaching at Union Theological Seminary in New York City, parallels Maguire's essay from another perspective. Rasmussen begins by pointing to the geological significance of the cliffs of the New Jersey palisades visible from the Manhattan side of the Hudson River. These majestic cliffs represent a rift in what millennia ago was a unified global continent, Pangaea. When this unified land base of earth tore apart into separate continents, separating Europe from the Americas and from Asia, these distinct regions entered into separate evolutionary histories. Different ecologies and cultures evolved in these separate world regions.

Then some five hundred years ago this regional separation began to be knit together by the conquering energies of the people of one particular region, England and Western Europe. These people sent their swarming population across all the other regions of the world as explorers, conquerors, and settlers and in the process not only reshaped the demography, but the ecology of all the other regions of the earth.

A vast genocide of peoples and destruction of their distinct ecologies ensued, as the wars and diseases brought by Europeans killed peoples who had evolved in other regions without experience of these diseases and instruments of violence. The biota brought by the Europeans included not only their microbes, but other flora and fauna, their livestock and grains, reshaping the ecology of these regions into Neo-Europes, marginating or destroying the distinct ecologies that had grown up in these regions in their separate histories.

To the agricultural revolution which had begun in the five to ten millennia before Christ in several distinct regions, the Europeans added the industrial revolution, financed by the vast wealth accrued through colonial conquest of these other lands. Although human population growth had begun slowly with the agricultural revolution ten thousand years ago, the population explosion is a phenomenon of the last two hundred years, based on the vast expansion of productivity created by the industrial revolution, together with successes in sanitation and medicine that doubled life expectancy for these growing populations.

The Christian religion played a major role in justifying this expansive European imperialism, as European Christians identified themselves with the God who shaped and ruled the whole world at will. The information revolution in the twentieth century extends this global reach of Europeanized domination over the people and resources of the earth, while accentuating the docetic abstraction of intellectual elites from the material connections of body and earth that underlie these resources.

For Rasmussen this combination of population, consumption, and waste is on a collision course with a limited earth, but the peoples of the Neo-Europes who continue to profit from it, while more and more other people and the earth grow impoverished, are unwilling to accept the depth of the reversal of both thought and social patterns necessary. Two alternatives stand in stark contrast: the ideology of "sustainable development" of United Nations and World Bank rhetoric that believes one can continue to expand but in a "sustainable way" and the revolt against this global domination of the dominant economic powers represented by the indigenous peoples of Chiapas.

The indigenous people of Chiapas represent the rise of the suppressed peoples and lands of alternative regions of Pangaea overwhelmed for five hundred years and more by the neo-Europeans. They ask, not for more "development" from these governments and their economic agents, but the right to control their own region shaped by indigenous customs and communal ecological patterns.

Rasmussen offers policy suggestions for the solution of this conflict, and suggests that something like greater accountability to local communities and the reintegration of society into its ecological base must be part of that fourth revolution the depths of whose demands continue to be resisted by those determined to pursue the trajectory of global expansion of the few against the many.

Whither both religious ethics and global policies that seek an ecologically sustainable earth community? Maguire and Rasmussen, while offering some elements of a solution,

go on to call the reader to dig into their own imaginations and
moral energies to make real commitments necessary to take
the problem itself seriously. Metanoia, change of consciousness, is necessary to inspire the will to real alternatives. The
religious communities have been part of the problem, but are
being called on to become sources of the spiritual energy that
must underlie any real commitment to a redemptive transformation.

MORE PEOPLE: LESS EARTH
THE SHADOW OF MAN-KIND

DANIEL C. MAGUIRE

Once again, a flight into Egypt was rich in symbol. Like the tense journey reported in Matthew's Gospel, anxious travelers made their way to Egypt in August 1994, in an effort to escape from peril and needless death. "Fear has large eyes," says an old Russian proverb, and twenty thousand representatives of the human race, eyes appropriately widened by fear, betook themselves to the United Nations International Conference on Population and Development (ICPD) in Cairo to try to save a world in terminal peril.

To call our peril "terminal" is not overwrought apocalypticism. The facts of our peril are as clear as the sun, but, like the sun, hard to look at for very long. And so we turn away and distract ourselves. At this epochal point of human history, a short and memorable catechism of the basic gory facts is essential intellectual and ethical equipment. To do this without numbing the mind with statistics is a dicey pedagogical challenge. So first to the plight of the earth and its nearly six billion denizens, and then to the theories and symbols to which the powerful, male-dominated Western world has too long been liege to its undoing.

A SHORT EARTH-CRISIS PRIMER

Oysters might be a fine place to start a basic catechism of earth-woes. The fabled Chesapeake Bay once enjoyed a thorough filtration by the massive oyster population every three days. Thus cleansed, the Bay flourished. Now the oysters are so depleted that the filtration occurs only a few times a year with portentous results. Similarly, mussels, as they busily glean vast quantities of water to glen out microscopic plankton, perform the filtering process for inland waters in the United States. Seventy-seven percent of them are either extinct or endangered.[1]

All life depends on cropland and on the earth's generous waters. As Timothy Wirth says in the language of business, "The economy is a wholly owned subsidiary of the environment."[2] Topsoil, that precious and thin layer of life support, is "washing like blood" into the seas and rivers.[3] In thirty years, China, where one of five humans lives, lost in cropland the equivalent of all the farms in France, Germany, Denmark, and the Netherlands. In fact, 43 percent of the earth's vegetated surface is to some degree degraded, and it takes from three thousand to twelve thousand years to develop sufficient soil to form productive land.[4]

All of China's major rivers are polluted. Less than 1 percent of the earth's water is usable by humans, and it is unevenly distributed. Most of Africa, the Near East, northern Asia, and Australia suffer from chronic water shortages. Water wars may be in our near future.[5]

And the richness of the seas is spoiling like the land. Of the 17 major world fisheries, 9 are in decline and all the others are threatened by unsustainable fishing practices. As far as the analysts' eyes can see into the future, we are faced with declining supplies of fish per person. Indeed, per capita supplies of water, fish, meat, and grain are declining.[6] Nineteen ninety-six marked the third straight year in which the world's grain harvest is below consumption, drawing down grain stocks to the lowest level on record. Meanwhile, the 1.6 percent yearly increase in world population requires 78,000 metric tons of grain per day just to stay at current consumption levels. Any shopper knows that means steadily rising costs of grain, and the hungry know that that means more hunger.

Not surprisingly, people, in solidarity with the decedent earth, are dying too. When it comes to impoverishment, the rule seems to be *women and children first!* Four million babies die yearly from diarrhea in the euphemistically entitled "developing world." Dr. Noeleen Heyzer of the United Nations says: "Poverty has a female face." Women constitute 70 percent of the world's 1.3 billion absolute poor, own less than 1 percent of the world's property but work two thirds of the world's working hours. In parts of Africa, only 18 percent of the people have access to clean drinking water. Seventy percent of the children in Upper Egypt suffer from water-related diseases. It has been said that if one glass of pure water was the cure for AIDS, most people in the world would not have access to it. Every year, up to sixty million people die from hunger related causes and over a billion people lack the calories for an active working life.[7] Microbes and viruses that found a life for themselves in the forests, have accepted deforesting humans as their new hosts. As Joel Cohen says: "The wild beasts of this century and the next are microbial, not carnivorous."[8] More than thirty new diseases have been identified since 1973, many of them relating to our new and ecologically dangerous lifestyles.[9]

Meanwhile, there are more of us. It took 10,000 generations to reach the first 2-1/2 billion; it took one generation to double it. Till the middle of the next century, the momentum is unstoppable. Overall fertility rates have been declining over the past forty years, but mortality rates are dropping even faster, and so our numbers inexorably grow.

World population is like a triangle, with the reproductive young at the wide base and the old at the narrow top. Until the model comes closer to a rectangle, with a more balanced distribution of young and old, the growth will not stop, and no one expects it to.

A new Mexico is added every year; a new China every ten years. *And over 90 percent of the growth is in the poorest parts of the world.* (In ironic witness to the current tragic inevitability, over two million were added to the world's numbers during the 1994 Cairo population conference itself.)

The United States is in no position to lecture the rest of the world on this. At the current rate of increase we add a Connecticut every year and a California every ten years.

As David Ben Gurion of Israel was wont to say, there are no experts on the future. Yet technology has made ethics more and more responsible for the future and its children, and so the effort to probe our demographic prospects is on. Optimists say we may cap growth at eight billion by the middle of the next century. The "worst-case" scenario envisioned at the United Nations—if everything goes wrong—is twenty-eight billion by the year 2150! That, of course, is an abstract estimate. With such growth the frustrations of nature would step in and cruelly limit births for us, striking first, as it has already begun to do, in the poorest parts of the world. (It is no longer meaningful, I submit, to divide the world up numerically into first, second, third, etc. If we insist on the numbers we would have to admit that there are third world sections in both the first and second world. Also the terms "developed" and "developing" house ungrounded assumptions about what "development" should be. It is, after all, the ecological barbarians of the world who refer to themselves as "developed." Enough said.)

NATIONS AS PARABLES

Population discussions are usually oversimplified. The problem is reduced to mathematics; there are too many people. By that is usually implied, too many poor people. "The untrammeled copulation of the poor" has been cited as the root of the whole difficulty. As a cure for Western myopia and lack of sophistication in this regard, a trip abroad is a necessary adjunct to our primer. Egypt and China, unlikely as they may appear, are my candidates. They may seem too dissimilar to be of any use, but let us see.

EGYPT AS MIRROR AND PORTENT

As our plane descended toward the Cairo airport, the scene out the window was one of death. Parched desert without a living leaf or twig in sight. How could fifty-eight million people live here? Of course, they cannot live on 96 percent of their land. All are huddled next to the polluted Nile on the 4 percent of somewhat habitable and arable land. And here the plot thickens and the apparently unique land of Egypt becomes a parable of us all.

On a traditional diet, Egypt could feed all its people. However, as Faiza Rady writes in the Egyptian publication *Al-Ahram*, "Egypt today grows more food for livestock than for people."[10] This is to feed the appetites for meat among Egypt's small elite. The results are predictable. A Study by the Massachusetts Institute of Technology and Cairo University reports that in Upper Egypt 83 percent of the children up to age five are malnourished, with 27 percent of them showing evidence of third-degree (severe) malnutrition. In Cairo, 80 percent of the children under two and 90 percent of the pregnant women are anemic.[11] Meanwhile, the distribution of land is becoming more inequitable under "structural adjustment" privatization schemes that favor the large landholders and increase the number of landless peasants. These *"development" refugees*—and note this: the world is filling with refugees from what we affluent folks call *development*—these development refugees move in desperation into the bulging cities, especially Cairo, which is now over fifteen million. It is said that one person is born in Cairo every minute and two arrive by train.

So Egypt first of all exemplifies maldistribution and its killing consequences. Some consolers like to stress that overall, global statistics are heartwarmingly hopeful. Overall food production on the earth is up, food prices are down, the fresh water supplies of the earth could meet the needs of up to twenty billion people. But to the water-poisoned and hungry of Cairo and the world those rosy statistics are a cruel and mocking abstraction. Sixty percent of the world's arable land lies in just twenty-nine countries where only 15 percent of the world's population live.[12] If population were redistributed to ease the pressure points, we could all have adequate diets, but are Kansas and Iowa, for example, ready to welcome five to ten million Bangladeshis to bring this about? (Ask the repatriated Haitian refugees about the American welcome for people of color.)

The implicit assumption animating much of the literature of consolation is that if the poor nations could get their act together they could eat as we eat. Wrong. This simply ignores the natural limits of this planet. In concrete terms, if China were to consume seafood at the same rate that the Japanese do, China would need the entire annual world fish catch![13] A recent study argues that no more than two billion people on planet earth could enjoy the North American diet, which derives 30 percent of its calories from animal sources. A South American diet, which derives 15 percent of its calories from animal sources, could sustain only four billion people. Six billion people could be nourished properly on a vegetarian diet if no grains were diverted to livestock.[14]

Of course, these are abstractions. They imagine a world of egalitarian sharing such as never has existed. What does exist, as historian Paul Kennedy observes, is a world in which "poverty has always existed yet never persuaded the rich to curb their life-styles in favor of the poor. . . ."[15] No one expects a miracle of compassion and sacrificial sharing from the well-heeled. What can be argued is that the price of not sharing may outweigh the price of continued insentient gluttony. Increasingly, the poverty of the poor encroaches. Businesses speak of "globalization," little noticing that the effects of poverty have also transcended borders. The damaging outreach of poverty has also been globalized. Through unwanted and unstoppable immigration, environmental degradation affecting climate and world food supply, terrorism and wars of redistribution—through all of this the poor, as never before in history, can hurt all of the rich.[16]

Enter, the Military

All of the above leads quite naturally to the soldiers. Egypt is an armed camp, with soldiers and police everywhere. Metal detectors greet you at the door of every hotel. Guards with submachine guns ride on tourist buses. Police boats accompany luxury cruises on the Nile. Some enemies of the status quo have turned to violence; these are invariably called "extremists" in the world press, and perhaps properly so. Curiously, those who preserve an unjust status quo with its greater violence are never called "extremists." In effect, we distinguish between respectable and unrespectable murder. Murder by economic and political arrangement is so familiar as not to seem extreme.

No external enemy threatens Egypt. The army that Egypt cannot afford is the military buttress of the status quo. Accordingly a crucial principle suggests itself: *Maldistribution always requires a military base.*

Within nations as varied as Egypt, Nigeria, Guatemala, Haiti, or North Korea the military are primarily a police force to contain an offended and exploited populace. Internationally, military arrangements seek to guarantee (for the benefit of the elite) structures marked by excessive wealth built on a base of excessive poverty. (The United States gives $2.1 billion in annual aid to Egypt, of which $1.3 billion is military assistance! *Washington Post,* Jan. 8, 1995, p. A-30. Military, *yes;* anemic children, *no,* seems the implicit American motto.)

The main function of any military is not to redress violations of human rights. There are other ways to do that and, as seen in Bosnia, the world's military did not feel called to rush nobly into human rights vindication, even when the violations were genocidal terrorism and widespread strategic rape. No, the most common military function is the preservation of privilege. Iraq and Kuwait have oil which undergirds the comfort and consumption patterns of the rich and so mobilization for "the Gulf war" was an instinctive reflex reaction fueled by popular enthusiasm. There was no felt need for the years of agonizing that gave protective covering to the Bosnian Serbs, allowing them to wax genocidal.

So Egypt is anything but an atypical troubled foreign land. It is, *mutatis mutandis,* a mirror image of ourselves. Egypt illustrates that "the population problem" is not a discrete, separable entity, but a network of consanguineous problems, none of which will be solved if the others are neglected. The population problem is not just numbers, though numbers count. Indeed with all its distinctness, the Egyptian paradigm all too nicely illustrates the six most common interrelated social mischiefs that underlie the ruination of the earth and its peoples. These are:

1. Maldistribution: the percolation of privilege to the top. Capitalism functions as a religion and an ethic for the gluttons of the earth. As David Loy points out, a pervasive and raw kind of capitalism "has become the most successful religion of all time, winning more converts more quickly than any previous belief system or value-system in the history of humanity."[17] This new religion even has the power to overwhelm the gentler streams of the tenured religions in lands it invades, religions such as Islam, Judaism, and Christianity. The rarely articulated but pervasively influential Golden Rule of this capitalism is that "the market" determines what is sacred and what is not, and clearly the poor, the good earth, and workers do not qualify as sacred. Social and distributive justice do not rank high in the pantheon of this new world religion.

This capitalistic religion supports the royal priesthood of the elite. As Egypt nicely illustrates the elite eat and the poor perish. All the earth-people are indeed in a ravenous frenzy of consumption. As Alan Durning points out, "The world's people have consumed as many goods and services since 1950 as all previous generations put together."[18] But the consuming is unequal and dirty. The well-to-do top fifth use 66 percent of the world's resources and generate 75 percent of the world's wastes and pollutants, including 96 percent of its radioactive wastes, and nearly 90 percent of ozone-depleting chlorofluorocarbons.[19]

The kind of capitalism that drives the world's globalizing economy today has more in common with the self-serving and arrogant religion of the ancient pharaohs than it dare pause to contemplate. The globalization of the economy is transferring power from governments (whose natural business is concern for the common good), to corporations whose concern is for the bottom line.

> Here is the pyramid to dwarf all pyramids. Profits and power shift to the small elite at the pharaohnic top and the increasing numbers of poor and the environment are unrepresented.[20]

2. This perversion of power leads to the second and related social mischief. National government is substantially perverted into the service of the elite, both within the country and in the international corporate high-priesthood.
3. Gross inequities cannot be supported democratically. Unfair distributional patterns can only be supported by force and deception. Thus, a military support system to contain the effects of this inequity is the corollary of social injustice.
4. Another hallmark of the current world economy is male dominance and the suppression of women. Systemically disempowered, the rate of female illiteracy is twice that of men in Egypt. The veiling and genital mutilation of women in Egypt perfectly and cruelly symbolize what we work to do to women in other cultures. The Western shock at these practices is rich in hypocrisy since we seem to feel no little horror at Western modes of social and psychological female mutilation.
5. Indifference is the cement of any unjust system. What is true for Egypt is commonplace. There is a lack of moral solidarity from other nations of the world who practice collective egoism. It is not considered a serious breach of international etiquette or law for nations to practice internal murderous neglect of the poor and disempowered groups. It would be a diplomatic *faux pas* even to raise such human rights issues, an intrusion into the "internal affairs" of sovereign states to suggest that the lethal suppression of groups within nations has anything substantive

to do with other nations' "national interest." Again, exemplifying this, the maintenance of a large army in Egypt is seen to be in the national interest of the United States, but the water poisoning of Egyptian children is not. Our aid allocation embodies precisely this barbaric message. Our commitment is to the elite, not to the children and adults pathetically scavenging in Egypt's dumps.

6. Finally, social devastation is furthered by the lack of family planning, abortion services, and good sex education. Hundreds of millions of women who want fertility regulation are denied the means for this by poverty, by indifference, and by the noxious influence of archaic religious taboos.

If all six of these ills are not seriously treated, the earth will increasingly be marked by unnecessary death.

CHINA AND THE DRACONIAN CRITICAL MASS

China also mirrors broader problems. It raises for us the question of the role of government in population policy. May government coerce if worst comes to worst? Could it, at least create *incentives*? Should it merely try to educate and plead? Or should government keep its hands off the sacred rights of reproduction and consider the right to have children a purely private choice to be made by a woman in consultation with her mate?

In much population discussion, and certainly at the 1994 United Nations conference in Cairo, the *c* word was taboo. The Cairo *Program of Action* says that in reproductive matters, "any form of coercion has no part to play."[21] It lumps "coercion" in with "discrimination" and with "violence" as infractions of human rights and the document even speaks disparagingly of social and economic "incentives and disincentives that affect individual decisions about child-bearing and family size."[22] The *Program of Action* is libertarian here though it does hope that those "individual decisions" will be free and responsible.[23] Sharon Camp speaks for this wide libertarian consensus when she writes: "There are no ethical or programmatic justifications for compulsory birth control, mandatory limits on family size, or artificial economic incentives and disincentives to discourage childbearing."[24] No compulsion, no mandatory limits, no incentives or disincentives. In other words, in the jargon of ethics, pressure, even in the softer form of incentives, is a "negative absolute." In this broad consensus *any* limitation of freedom is taboo.

Obviously, deceptive birth-limiting practices that damage women's health are morally outrageous, as are denials of basic sustenance and health care to force sterilization of the poor. Denial of housing that punishes the already born children admits of no ethical defense. Also, we must face the question of how much of China's success in containing births is due to repression and how much is due to other factors.[25] We must also look at success in other poor nations where governmental pressures are not a significant factor, as in the Indian state of Kerala. However, the position that governmental and sociocultural pressures have had no influence whatever on fertility control in China is unproved and unprovable. Indeed, by some estimates, 240 million more Chinese would have been born over the last two decades without the one-child policy.[26] As the study by Griffith Feeney and Wang Feng concludes, the drop from six children per woman before 1970 to near replacement level in 1990 "occurred far more rapidly than any other recorded country-level decline in history." They argue that over half of this decline was due to government intervention, and they note "general agreement among scholars that government policy has played a major role in China's fertility decline. . . ."[27]

Put another way, who would confidently defend the position that if all social constraints were removed there will be no demographic impact in China? Professor Amartya Sen who opposes any governmental pressure has to admit that the effect of incentives and coercion in China is "not clear."[28] Perhaps. But if it is "not clear" then it *might be* crucially influential. If it is not clear whether the fertility rate would have *decreased* without the social pressure it might have *increased.* The fertility rate was 2.8 in 1979 in China when the one-child policy came into effect; it is approaching 1.9 in the early 1990s.

In his book *Who Will Feed China?*, Lester Brown sounds a new note in population debate. He notes that Chinese leaders some twenty years ago analyzed future population, land, and water trends and realized that they had to choose between the reproductive rights of those now alive and the survival rights of the next generation. "What separates the government in Beijing from those in many other countries is that it is desperately trying to protect the options of the next generation, politically difficult though that may be. This farsightedness and the political courage of the government of China deserve recognition."[29] The Feeney-Feng study concurs: "The Chinese leadership has every reason to be satisfied with what has been accomplished in hastening fertility decline, hence slowing population growth in China."[30]

Also, a readiness to believe the worst of Communist regimes may have discolored a lot of reporting on the one-child policy. Studies of four rural counties conclude that press suggestions of draconian enforcement of the fertility policy and widespread use of coercive abortion are inaccurate. The real picture is one of a program that is more variable, flexible, and voluntary than commonly depicted.[31]

Is it possible that Western, and especially American, views of China may be more than a little elitist? As an exercise in moral imagination, ask yourself what would have happened if the Chinese students' revolution of 1989 had succeeded. Suppose the brave students we cheered as they faced the tanks had prevailed. One possible result is that, with all coercive restraints on reproduction suddenly dissolved in what many in the West assumed to be a hunger for individualistic freedom and libertarian capitalism, the demographic lid on one fifth of the world might have blown off! Is our love of freedom strong enough to welcome that? We deplore as "draconian" China's measures of birth limitation. However, as I asked in my address at the U.N. at the second preparatory committee meeting for the ICPD, could not China be teaching us "that you can arrive at a *draconian critical mass* where draconian measures are the last defense against disaster?" Could China, as portent, be saying to us "choose justice and sanity before coercion or incentives are all you have left?"[32]

I repeat, some coercive methods used in China would be defended by no one. Other methods of strong social persuasion have deep roots in Chinese culture and the case has not been made that all of these methods are malignant. As professor Luo Ping, sociologist and director of the Women's Studies Center at Wuhan University, cautions Western critics regarding China's family planning goals: "Family planning must be implemented in a country like China where the size of the population puts too much pressure on the economy and on society. . . . China is just like a small boat which can only carry 100 people but already has 110 in it."[33]

It is true that other factors such as economic improvement and urbanization have influenced Chinese birth limitation but often at considerable cost to the ecology.[34] At the least, it should be seen that the issue is complex and that the Cairo dogma painting everything down to persuasion and incentives as intrinsically evil and unworthy of a hearing is simplistic. The China experience is an urgent invitation to revisit the question of the proper role of public policy and government in population matters. It is also the time to press the question of just what government is and what its legitimate and ever-changing roles are in the development of a just society and just world.[35] But first to the miracle of Kerala, a success-without-coercion story.

KERALA VERSUS CHINA

The Indian state of Kerala is a stunning success story. While its poverty rate is worse than the average in India, Kerala's fertility rate is 1.8 and its fertility rate is falling faster than the fertility rate in the United States. The life expectancy for a Keralite male is seventy, while that of a North American male is only seventy-two. The typical marrying age in Kerala is twenty-two as opposed to eighteen in the rest of India. The life expectancy of women in Kerala exceeds that of men, just as in the affluent world. There is a systematic attempt in Kerala to achieve "land literacy" as well as word literacy, so that soil conservation is studied and effectively taught.

This is credited to the powerful tradition of participatory democracy in Kerala nourished by literacy—Kerala is less caste-ridden than any other part of the Hindu world—and especially by the strong and long term commitment to women's education. Female literacy is 87 percent compared to 68 percent in China. The dropout rate for girls from grades one to five is an almost unbelievable *zero percent* and some districts of Kerala have recently celebrated 100 percent literacy. All this is done without any state coercion.

Amartya Sen makes much of this in his critique of China's pressuring one-child policy and it is tempting to join him.[36] Who would not prefer freedom to pressure when freedom works! However, Kerala achieves the empowerment of women through distinctive participatory democratic social processes and education, all of this rooted in a deep cultural commitment to these and other social values. Bill McKibben, author of *The End of Nature*, attributes Kerala's success to a "quartet of emancipations": they have freed themselves from the worst of caste distinctions, religious bigotry, illiteracy, and gender discrimination.[37] If, in these regards, the world were Kerala writ large, we would have no problem. If China were Kerala we would have no problem.

And there is the rub. It is not. Kerala is infused with an intense and special sense of democracy and passion for dialogue. It voted Communist power in and out again and has complex political and religious coalitions working and interlocking in its political economy. Culturally and historically Kerala and China are not a match and therefore it is a nonsequitur to transmute Kerala into a principle condemning all incentive programs in other contexts. One successful *is* does not create a universal *ought*.

Of course, the "one family, one child" policy in China

may become moot if the economic and political changes begun in 1979 continue. These trends run counter to the needs of a controlled society. They have already sent almost 10 percent of the population into internal diaspora. In what has been described as "the largest mass migration in recent human history," people are fleeing to the cities. And that migration is just beginning. While providing cheap labor to the burgeoning coastal economy, these "floaters" "are seriously undermining the government's ability to carry out such crucial national programs as its 'one family, one child' policy." These are the words of Orville Schell, a longtime China observer, now at Columbia University.[38] Add to this the apparently unstoppable regionalization and decline of federal control in China, and we may soon have empirical evidence of what happens when the controversial controls abate.

GOVERNMENT AS AN ISSUE OF ETHICS

One day in a simpler time, Thomas Aquinas sat down to comment on Aristotle's *Politics*. Thomas agreed with Aristotle that the number of children generated should not exceed the resources of the community and that this should be ensured by law as needed. Thomas eschewed the suggestion that homosexuality be used for birth limitation, but he did not shrink from the need for the state to limit birth. If more than a determined number of citizens were generated, he, said, the result would be poverty which would breed thievery, sedition, and chaos.[39] As Johannes Messner says, it is "not without surprise that one finds St. Thomas suggesting the restriction of procreation after a certain number of children."[40] I would add, it is even more surprising to find Thomas intimating the need for pressure or coercion by the state. Thomas is talking law, and law requires sanctions to be effective. At what point of crisis do we declare some sanctions draconian? That question survived Thomas (who sidestepped it) and confronts us, shy from it though we may. At the barest minimum it should stir us to heroic efforts to avoid the draconian bind. It challenges our confidence in the

libertarian absolute that government has nothing whatever
to say or do about the common good being suffocated by an
insupportable increase in population. (Interestingly, and
equally surprisingly, John Stuart Mill in his paean to liberty
also defended legal restraints against the "serious evil" of
overpopulation.)[41]

One thing is clear in conclusion: freedom of choice in
reproductive matters, given their intimacy and personal significance, is the ideal. But personhood is conceived and nourished in community, and community entails social obliga-
tions and debts. Personal rights, however cherished, may
need to be curtailed by the essential requirements of the
common good. We admit this principle readily in other contexts. Western individualists—lacking a coherent philosophy
of the common good—almost deify the right to private property and the right to make personal consumption choices.
Yet, slowly and reluctantly, these same theory-poor individualists have conceded that the common good demands that we
curtail some personal "rights." We limit the "right" to burn
lead in our cars and leaves in our yards, and factories are
blocked from polluting air, water, and soil. Serious policy
options today include forcing companies to recycle their
products (such as television sets and cars) after they are worn
out by the purchasers. The cost of this should be reflected in
the original purchase price in a way that allows the consumer
to share in but not shoulder the full recycling burden. Green
taxes to reward the nonpolluters suddenly make sense. The
moral and political principle in all of this is that *individual
choices may be limited as required by the common good.*
And government by definition is the primary overseer of the
common good. This does not of course mean that we should
sit and wait until government tells us what to do. Social justice is the term for our debts to the common good and those
debts should be paid in an ongoing manner. We should not be
waiting for government to tell us to curb our meat-eating,
waste-making ways. The hunger of the poor and the limits of
the earth should speak to our consciences before government
has to. It is, however, our moral callousness and egoism that

make even more necessary the natural role of government as prime overseer of the common good.

The application of this to reproductive choice is a tenderness we affluent nations would rather not probe.

WHAT IS GOVERNMENT?

The purpose of government as *the prime caretaker of the common good and the prime protector of the disempowered* requires it to preserve conditions where human and biological life can survive and thrive.[42] Where personal conscience and voluntarism are inadequate, we make laws and we enforce them. This is basic social justice theory and common practice. Has it no application at all to reproductive choices? Reproductive choices affect our ecology and societal viability. Government and law must address that.

THE ALTERNATIVES TO PRESSURE

The ICPD in Cairo, though it overstated the case, was sensibly anxious to keep reproductive choices as free as possible. Though not all of these points made it into the final document—indeed some are sadly missing or underplayed—there was strong agreement in that marvelous assembly on the following antidotes to the diseases of a failing earth. Indeed, had the nongovernmental organizations (the NGOs) been allowed to draft the *Program of Action* free of the antiquarian wrangles of the officials, the document could have been a classic. Even in its present form, however, it is a moral masterpiece. There was broad agreement at Cairo on the following:

1. The empowerment of women. This has happily become the dominating theme of population discussions. The purpose of this is not to substitute matriarchy for patriarchy but to promote the empowerment of all people, including neglected indigenous people, in increasingly democratic and collegial social structures.

2. universal and effective care of children.

3. development redefined to include primary reference to the elimination of poverty and to the primacy of earth-cherishing.

4. the taming of consumption by the affluent, especially the profligate consumptions of parasitical military establishments. In this regard it is essential to note that consumption patterns must be factored into the definition of overpopulation. In this sense, the United States is the most populated nation in the world since our 2.1 superconsumers per family are the equivalent of some 30 to 40 consumers per family in the poor world. Add to this our unbridled passion for military spending and international arms sales and we in the United States have impressive reasons to claim the title of the world's worst offender against the security of the planet. (Strangely, American religions and other moral instructors have not tried to define *saving the planet* as a "family value." Again *individualism* and a diminished sense of the *common good* dim the optic nerve.)

5. reverence for our parental earth and the limits it puts to growth, using *biocentric* rather than *anthropocentric* criteria.

6. contraception and safe abortion. It was said in the past that development is the best contraceptive. Actually, development that does not eliminate poverty may not be any kind of a contraceptive. Hope is the best contraceptive. And without all six of these points there is no hope. Without *all* of the above, incentives, if not coercion in some form, may be our destiny.

RELIGIONS IN THE NEXT MILLENNIUM

In one sense, the Cairo conference was an invitation to religious prophecy. With occidental skittishness, the word *religion* was slighted in the official *Program of Action* but the best values of the world's major religions pervaded the final product. Understandably, press attention was given to the Vatican's idiosyncratic fixation on debatable issues of reproductive ethics and to its newfound friendship with some parts of Islam. Clearly this Vatican-Islamic alliance did not relate, as alleged, to abortion. Abortion coexisted with the Vatican and Islam for fourteen centuries and yielded no ecumenical coziness. No, the new tactical alliance more plausibly resulted from a new and common threat nervously perceived by these two patriarchies—*the rise of womankind.* However, this Vatican-orchestrated pugnacious pageantry was sideshow.

In fact, many of the best values of Judaism, Christianity, Islam, and other world religions are enshrined in that final ICPD document. I attended the Cairo conference with a newly formed group known as The Religious Consultation on Population, Reproductive Health and Ethics. This international, multireligious group of scholars and leaders was formed in the conviction that the moral energies of the world's religions are renewable and applicable to the contemporary terracidal crisis. The Consultation, with representatives from Judaism, Christianity, Islam, Buddhism, Hinduism, and other religions found a hunger for alternative religious voices of a progressive sort. While originally scheduled to conduct one Non-Governmental Organization (NGO) session, doors kept opening to us and our members ended up doing seven sessions and giving one address to the plenary of the U.N. nations. This was symbolic of what other religious groups found, a desire to hear constructive alternative voices from the world's religions on the problems of population, consumption, and ecology. The 1992 "Warning to Humanity" signed by 1,600 scientists, including 102 Nobel Laureates, called on religious communities to rise to meet the challenge to our planet. If the world's religions can reverse the fossilization process to which many have succumbed and rise to this occasion, an audience awaits.

RELIGION: THE PROSPECTS FOR REVOLUTION AND RENAISSANCE

The world's religions are and will be players in the population, ecology, and consumption issues. Two thirds of the world population are mentally and emotively linked to these powerful symbol systems. (Even the avowedly secular are under the spell of these ideological, culture-permeating symbol-generators.) The only question is whether the religious influences will be noxious or helpful.

There are two distinct challenges facing these religions in the dawning millennium. The first is already meeting with some success. The second challenge, I will argue, is more daunting and has hardly been addressed.

The first challenge is to speak to those who function within the traditional symbolic meaning-systems and imaginal fields of the world's religions, that is, "the faithful." Here reformers are mining their traditions, filtering out the poisons that inevitably accrued and directing the purified power of these imperfect but powerful moral classics to our demagogic and ecological predicament.

Professor Riffat Hassan was warmly appreciated at the Cairo conference when she said that she could go into her native Pakistan with the U.N. *Program of Action* in hand and get no hearing at all, but that if she went in with the *Program* in one hand and the Qur'an in the other, she would be welcomed, heard, and understood. She and other scholars like her mine the Qur'an to empower women. She brought Muslim women to their feet when she said: "I urge all Muslim women present to take your destiny into your own hands. Once you know what your rights are and that they are given to you by God, you will never let any man in any society take them away from you again." Azizah al-Hibri told an ICPD preparatory NGO meeting at the United Nations: "The majority of Muslim scholars permit abortion, although they differ on the state of fetal development beyond which it becomes prohibited."[43] She stated a similar position on contraception.

Even in the Islamic Republic of Iran, there is an influential, religiously grounded women's movement promoting the empowerment of women and family planning. As Homa Hoodfar writes: "The advantage of the new Islamist feminists over more secularized 'Western' activists is that they challenge and reform the Islamic doctrine from within rather than advocating a Western model of gender relations."[44] And, regarding the ability of these reformers to squeeze new wine from old wineskin, Nikki Keddie says in defense, that their new "interpretations of Islam are no more forced than our Supreme Court's varying interpretations of the U.S. Constitution."[45] As is ever the case, the rise of women is the rise of hard questions. The Egyptian feminist Aida Seif al-Dowla, asks: "Why is it easier to insert Norplant in a woman's arm than to tell a man in Mohandissin not to drive his Mercedes?"[46]

Tradition-based religious reformers are having success elsewhere. It has been an imperative of some Chinese religions to preserve the patrilinear family. As Harold Coward writes: "If there is not a son to conduct the family rituals then the parents, grandparents, etc. will cease to exist upon the last son's death and the family will come to an end." Reformers have so changed things that it is now widely accepted that a girl could also perform these saving rituals.[47]

Workshops on how to wrench the new from the old are ongoing in the Christian base communities of Latin America. Elements in the Hindu tradition that urged conservation and respect for nature are being revitalized.[48] Scholars in Judaism and Buddhism are retrieving the neglected resources in those traditions that speak helpfully to population, consumption, and ecology.[49] Catholics for a Free Choice, with affiliates in Washington, Montevideo, Mexico City, and San Paolo is successfully educating Catholics on progressive ideas in their tradition regarding reproductive ethics and the empowerment of women. Religions reach into the center of human personality, to the motivational core where the sense of the sacred pulses. No realistic study of power or social change can afford to miss that.

DE-ORPHANING RELIGION

The efforts at creative traditionalism are heartening and necessary. Since the world's religions are the lenses through which so many see reality, those seeking to redirect the all too latent moral energies of these cultural powerhouses to our planetary predicament are doing good work. The tougher problem that challenges those who recognize the power of religion is to reach those for whom those old forms do not speak, the secularists (with their social science priesthood) who hold most of the power in most of the world and who are appallingly innocent of the role of the religiosacred in social psychology. Their orthodoxy ignores the fact that religion is an ubiquitous mover and shaker in the body politic. Even those who are not explicitly plugged into a named religious grouping hold some values sacred and are therefore part of the religious phenomenon.

It is no easy thing to charge sophisticates with naïveté. Yet this is the capital sin of most who hold the imperium in modern political and economic discourse. Their naïveté, which is vague about ethics and uses "theological" as a pejorative term, treats religion as an irrelevancy. The error here is crude. To speak of statecraft and ignore religion is to speak of marriage while ignoring sex. There is more to marriage than sex and more to politics than religion, but separation is a fantasy.

A recently published book *Religion, the Missing Dimension of Statecraft* focuses on the world's institutionalized religions and gives numerous case studies of how American foreign policy failed by refusing to recognize the power of religious influences.[50] Whatever religion is it is power, and power brokers who disdain it are afflicted with impaired reality contact. Unfortunately, Wilfred Cantwell Smith was talking his good sense into a large Western secular void when he said: "The task of constructing even that minimum degree of world fellowship that will be necessary for [people] to survive at all is far too great to be accomplished on any other than a religious basis." [51] Also talking power, John Henry Newman said, people will die for a dogma who will not stir for a conclusion. Camus supports this practical observation when he remarks that no one is disposed to die for scientific truths. Values perceived as sacred are the ultimate motivators. Values worth dying for are what religion, at root, is all about. And there will have to be a lot of dying to solve the world's ecological and demographic problems—dying to privilege and to long, nasty habits of power and control. The problems outlined in the primer above are not patient of a technical fix. Flowcharts and cybertechnics will not turn the world on end or produce the needed cultural revolutions.

What is needed to stop the killing of the earth and its increasingly imperiled residents? Historically unparalleled revolutions and metamorphoses. As a United Nations report sums it up: "For ten thousand years, civil societies have almost invariably been structured *for* the principal benefit of a small proportion of their members."[52] A cure for the world's woes cannot be built on that tenured oligarchical tyranny, a tyranny that has only begun to be challenged in modern times.

There is an absolute necessity for an historically unparalleled panhuman solidarity, a dissolving of tribal nationalism, and an awakening of awe before the miracle of this earth. And that awe for the earth must be muscularized into law and into new economic arrangements and consumption habits. Men must share real power with women. The rich must forgive debts and share wealth with the poor as never before in history. The fervidly held idea that biological nature is an infinity made for us omnivorous human gobblers, must die. All that for starters!

Try any of the above without the values that people find sacred. And religion, by definition, refers to what people find sacred. Since religion is such a neglected category in the West, an analytical pause is in order.

WHAT IS RELIGION?

First of all, *where* is it? Religion is not confined to mosques, temples, shrines, churches, or to theism. Religion is panhuman because it is, essentially and definitionally, a *response to the sacred* and there is no one who finds nothing sacred. *Homo sapiens* is only sometimes *sapiens* but is always *homo sacralis.* Thales was right: everything is full of Gods! Social existence, said Alexis de Toqueville, falls apart without truths held as sacred. Not to know that is not to know how the human animal works. The occidental conviction that to be modern one must ignore the category of the sacred is institutionalized stupidity.

The "world religions" have no monopoly on the genus "religion." Since power is often most visible in its pathology—and religions are a form of power—we need only look at the ethnic battles in Africa, Eastern Europe, Ireland, and the Middle East to see how sacralized values (enfleshed in nationalism) ignite the soul.

Toynbee said that "religion is one of the essential faculties of human nature."[53] If people do not find it in one place, they will extract grains of it from the most unlikely ores. In modern supposedly democratic nations he concludes that "four-fifths of the religions of five-sixths of the population" is nationalism. As he puts it, the religion of the masses is but the "worship of the deified community concealed under the fine name of patriotism."[54] Rechanneling that power—and those misplaced sacreds—to social good is not an option; it is a necessity for survival. The sacred—however described, theistically or nontheistically—is the motor of all major cultural reform. To try to change culture with mere rationality is like writing a love letter with mathematical formulae. You will get nowhere. The population-ecology-consumption crisis will not be solved by nude rationality but only by truths that stir the flaccid collective will by touching the sacral core of human willing.

Though we are more familiar with religious power in its toxic forms, modern Western culture is less aware that it has been shaped by religiously borne values and symbols. The idea pioneered by the early Hebrews that the "image of God" is not found in princes but in ourselves and in our children is seen as the stimulus for modern democratic theory and for things as concrete as the American Bill of Rights.[55] As Elaine Pagels points out, the moral revolutions that came to be called Judaism and Christianity "forged the basis for what would become, centuries later, the western ideas of freedom and the infinite value of each human life."[56] In our secular modernity, religions suffer from a neurotic sense of inferiority. They forget the culture-changing successes they had in the past. As Garry Wills writes, most of the revolutionary movements that transformed, shaped, and reshaped the American nation—"abolitionism, women's suffrage, the union movement, the civil rights movement . . . grew out of religious circles."[57] Other religions have had similar influence. Tibetan Buddhism, for example, so changed culture and reversed history that it made more young men into monks than into soldiers. The Islamic influence on the politics and economics of cultures where it takes root is only now being belatedly appreciated in our religiously retarded social analysis. And so on.

Not only are religions powerful, but those modern thinkers who study religion and write on it acquire, by a kind of osmosis of power, high cultural impact. As professor Daniel Pals says, the ideas of those who interpret religion filter beyond the religious sphere and "affect our literature, philosophy, history, politics, art, psychology, and, indeed, almost every realm of modern thought."[58] Classical sociologists and historians who took the time to study it have recognized the culture-shaping power of religious forces, but much of Western thought is banefully innocent and possessed of an adolescent rebellious scorn in this regard.

Perhaps the fault for this does not fall on the shoulders of Western thinkers. It may, in the main, be God's fault. Or, rather, the fault of those men who fashioned and shaped the Western God.

As Jack Miles points out in his remarkable book, *God: A Biography,* the God-figure of the Jewish and Christian Bible became not only the major literary figure in the West, but, indeed, the very "mirror of the West" and a major determinant of its moral and political personality.[59] As far as social analysis goes, the avoidance of God-talk is a commitment to ignorance. Whether or not such a God "exists," the literary image of this God has been and is a major player for good and for ill in the shaping of Western culture, politics, and economics.

BEYOND LYNN WHITE

The masculine God of this literary production is complex and the ideals he embodies are not always benevolent influences on our politics or economics. Lynn White famously spotted biblical anthropocentrism as an ecological culprit. His criticism was that the biblical mandate to "fill the earth and master it" spawned Western society's "ruthlessness toward nature."[60] His critique was not so much wrong as superficial. The problems bequeathed to Western culture by the Hebrew and Christian traditions may be more serious than he knew. We have to ask whether the very basic symbols of biblical faith may be full of mischief, including the distinct existence of an actual personal being called "God." Theism itself may be a problem quite related to our world crisis. A world in terminal peril can rule no question out of order.

What happens when we see the world and say "God" rather than seeing it and saying "Wow!" Is *appreciation* shortcircuited by *ratiocination* and cause-effect calculation? Does creation theology not belittle nature by reducing this primal miracle to an artifact, prompting us to worship the purported cause while draining us of wonder at "the effect?" If the earth could speak, would it say it would have been better off without our distracting theism? Questions are decent. They fight fairly. And these are questions.

THE COGNITIVE STATUS OF GOD

Diagnosing and curing God-related mischief may require conversions of thought and a recasting of symbols that are too unpalatable to be undertaken. "People of the book," might be able to clean up many of their symbols and to change accents in their traditions, but around certain symbols, the theological wagons are drawn. Understandably, for many Christians, for example, serious questioning of a distinct existent called God, or of Jesus as an embodiment of this God, or of afterlife is not welcome.

Indeed the Abrahamic religions are notoriously unopen to dialogue about their beliefs. Among the classical civilizations of Greece and Rome, there was a kind of freewheeling democratic tolerance of diverse divinities and theologies. Herodotus (484–425 B.C.E.) evinced no sense of threat when he commented amiably that the Gods Amon and Horus that he met in Egypt were the equivalents of Zeus and Apollo from his native Greece. This same relaxed attitude is seen in Euhemerus (330–260 B.C.E.) who felt free to speculate that the Gods were simply historical persons who began to be worshiped after they died. Some of the Stoics could wonder whether the Gods might just be personifications of sea and sky and other natural forces and phenomena.

There was nothing freewheeling and tolerant about ancient Israel in this regard. Isaiah was not into genial dialogue with those who doubted that the Lord of the covenant had spoken to Abraham, Isaac, Jacob, and Moses. The Christian Paul said that even if an angel from heaven were to teach anything at variance with what he taught that even such a supernatural being should be considered an "outcast" (Galatians 1:8). The children of Israel, Christianity, and Islam all displayed this rigidity throughout most of their history. Those who took a different view of things religious were candidates for rack and stake, with hell fires the eternal sequel to their gory demise. This overconfident dogmatism, was an epistemological tone-setter in the formation of Western culture and, as Professor Pals writes, "came to dominate Western civilization throughout most of the medieval era."[61] And indeed as the West moved scientifically and philosophically from the medieval to the modern they did not easily shake off this habit of simplistic sureness. The current ill-defined "postmodernism" is a delayed adolescent rebellion against the pancertitudinalism that the Abrahamic religions bequeathed to the world.

The practical result of this for our purposes here is that the massive Abrahamic religions that dominate much of the world are still insensitive to religious and cultural diversity. Their theism particularly is not on the agenda for open discussion.

This is a major block to interfaith dialogue of the sort this planetary community requires. The nontheism of Buddhism, the
imaginative pluralism of Hindu theism, and the theistic role of
ancestors in many native religions jar the cocksure Abrahamic
perspective. A little modesty regarding the theistic claims of
Judaism, Christianity, and Islam is a precondition for cross-cul-
tural exchanges of the sort that our earth-crisis requires.

Perhaps this modesty is seeping in, almost quietly.
Strange to tell, welcome or not, traditional beliefs about God
factor less and less into the thinking even of contemporary
Christian theologians. God as a personal being is in the warp
and woof of an Aquinas or an Augustine as it is in the
thought of an Abraham Heschel or a Karl Barth. In these thor-
oughgoing theists, God is functionally present as the ultimate goal of all human willing. From their perspective if you
removed God from their theology the bottom would fall out.[62]
That is not true for many of today's theologians and religious
thinkers. God as the metaphoric embodiment of the moral
elan of the tradition is in place, but God as a distinct existent
Being is not a functional component of many contemporary
religious theorists. For them, the bottom would not fall out.
They write *quasi Deus non daretur*, as if God does not exist.

The long, central God-as-existent-person images may
also be slipping from popular consciousness which often runs
ahead of theory. Even though God in some form is still regularly thanked for touchdowns in the National Football
League, in the popular arena, the marginalization of the traditional "God" moves apace. It may be reflected in the remarkable exodus from the main-line churches.[63] It seems a lesson
of religious history that symbols must discover the vernacu-
lar of the time and be appropriately related and thus intelligi-
ble to the evolving consciousness and culture or they will be
shunted to a siding.

DIAGNOSING GOD

Douglas Meeks points to a problem in the dominant
divine figure of Western literary history. He argues that the

imagining of God as supreme master has helped shape the Western definition of human freedom as untrammeled mastery. If God is the masculinized owner of all he sees, and we, especially we men, are made in his image, what results? "In the West," Meeks writes, "this has been manifested in terms of the white male's mastery of nature, women, people of color, and his own body."[64] The assumed absolute supremacy of God tendentially belittles everything and everyone else. John Calvin said: "No heed is to be paid to humanity when the honor of God is at stake."[65] Another mischief is that belief in the divine providence of an almighty God who "orders all things benignly" can justify human improvidence.[66] Muck up the earth as we might, this all-provident Orderer will take care.

Further vexing God-questions press themselves on the modern mind. Could it be that the anti-ecological streams of biblical anthropocentrism—cited by Lynn White and others—are the natural issue of biblical monotheism? The anthropologist Loren Eiseley saw Christian monotheism as causing an epochal intellectual upheaval that did indeed prepare the way for the emergence of science. In this, as in all upheavals, something was gained and something was lost. The result was "a monotheistic reign of law by a single deity so that [humans] no longer saw distinct and powerful spirits in every tree or running brook."[67] This death of enchantment opened the way for the demeaning instrumentalization of nature and the human alienation from our biological matrix.

Also, could monotheism, with its lonely notion of a single, self-contained God, be seen as the ultimate symbol and reification of a social individualism? Did not Christians try to ease the pain of a solitary, isolated monotheistic God, in spite of all the theological caveats and cavils, by the postbiblical tritheism of trinitarian theology? No matter how the dons dunned on this, three never did equal one. Was this not really an effort to socialize the damage of a single, supreme, all-owning deity as the image of each of us, an image that conflicts with other stirring biblical images of our social solidarity? But now to an even more serious question.

DOES GOD EXIST?

It is good to acknowledge at the outset that this question can usher in a debate that no one can win. *If one accepts the question as legitimate,* there is no overwhelming proof in either direction. Even David Hume, who argued against the existence of a personal God, said that the argument for the existence of a God from the apparent design in nature is reasonable though inconclusive.[68] It can equally well be argued that the position on the nonexistence of such a God is also reasonable but inconclusive. Splendid arguments have been marshaled to prove that our reality is unintelligible without a God concept at its root. Clearly it would not seem senseless to posit a designer at the root of all the patterns and designs in nature, designs so complex and mysterious that science at its best can only seek to discover and mimic them. Thomas Aquinas put his finger on the main marvel of biology noting with wonder that those things that lack intelligence act purposefully. As G. K. Chesterton said, it would for him take too much faith to say there is no designer behind all this design.[69]

So theism is not *prima facie* unintelligent. It is, however, irreducibly pluralistic since the human imaginings of Gods are irrepressibly diverse. It is therefore a modest assertion to say that the human race will never be united (as it needs to be on a shrinking earth) by way of unanimity on the God-question.[70] Indeed, the pursuit of the question has tended to be more divisive and disruptive than unitive. God, however, cannot be ignored. Too much of the world's morality and culture is knit into God-talk and God-talk is a featured presence in conversations on population, ecology, and consumption. A hard critical look at the presuppositions behind the idea of an existing personal God is generally bypassed in modern secular culture out of politeness or indifference, but that is a default of nerve.

Let us try a different tack on the old question of whether God (or Gods) exists.

A NEW HYPOTHESIS

Rather than light on disagreements about the answers to the question *does God exist?*, I propose to question the question. It is hard for a question to be wrong, but this one might well be. Traditional answers accepted the presuppositions of the question; Theism said "yes!" Atheism said "no!" Agnosticism said "Who knows?" All miss the distinct possibility that the question may well be misplaced and misconceived, assuming as it does that God can be thought of as one among many *existents* . . . bigger, greater, better, more mysterious, more uppercase, but ultimately one of the bunch of discrete beings that exist. Labored efforts were of course made not to make God a capitalized member of the crowd of existing entities, because a God that is too much like the rest of us is not very godly. My hypothesis questions whether these labored efforts were fatally flawed from the start.

Notice then, that my hypothesis is more radical than the position of David Hume. He said the existence of such a *Deus Faber*, God as the manufacturer of our world, is not unreasonable, thus accepting that the question of God's existence is a fair one. I am suggesting that the very question is misconceived.

ANALOGY TO THE RESCUE?

The defenders of theism never lacked subtlety and they did not miss their need to avoid making God just one of our kind writ large. Trying to slip out of this anthropomorphic bind that theism faces, Augustine went so far as to say that in talking about God, if we have understood, then what we have understood is not God. *Si comprehendis, non est Deus.*[71] Fine, but putting God outside the realm of the understandable is the very definition of agnosticism. Thomas Aquinas said the highest form of knowledge of God is of God "as the unknown."[72] Agnostics, in their fashion, agree completely. Again, Aquinas: "Now we cannot know what God is, but only what God is not; we must therefore consider the ways in which God does not exist, rather than the ways in which God does."[73] Somewhat baffled at this point, the agnostics would still be nodding in agreement. A modern theologian, Elizabeth Johnson will add to their befuddlement, saying that "the reality of God is mystery beyond all imagining." And again: "God, then, is outside of all classes and categories and beyond the possibility of being imagined or conceived."[74] Sallie McFague joins in, insisting on the need for metaphor since all language about God is inadequate and all of it is improper.[75]

So, in sum, God is beyond knowing, beyond imagining, beyond understanding, beyond the grasp of language. Of course, these same theologians then go on to talk of God as lover, friend, parent, lawgiver, conversation partner, and all kinds of other quite understandable things. The ineffable becomes *effable*, the unimaginable is imagined in very specific terms and given a very distinct function and personality. After proclaiming utter incomprehensibility, they retreat to comprehensible anthropomorphisms—as though their expressed observations about the impossibility of this very thing excused their inconsistency. Admittedly, they are impaled on a mean paradox.

Humphrey Palmer sees the problem of theologians who want to speak of God as "totally different, but . . ." He writes: "If theologians use words in their ordinary sense, their theology will be anthropomorphic. If, on the other hand, a term is to mean something quite different when applied to God, then theology is incomprehensible."[76] Similarly, according to Ian Barbour, "If familiar terms are predicated of God literally (univocally), one ends in anthropomorphism. But if no familiar terms can be predicated, except equivocally, one ends in agnosticism. (If divine love in no way resembles human love, the term is vacuous.)"[77] Some theologians actually make the leap, speaking of God as an imaginative construct of human making, not as a distinct "being."[78] Indeed, the quiet metaphorization of God is well on. Is it possible, amid the raging love of *"post"* words among today's intellectuals, that there is a great deal of unconfessed posttheistic Christianity?

In 1942, Heinrich Zimmer wrote that "we of the Occident are about to arrive at a crossroads that was reached by the thinkers of India some seven hundred years before Christ." This crossroads, he continues, is a *nontheistic* reassessment of the world "that we ourselves are on the point of reaching today in the West, if indeed we are not already there."[79] Forty years later James Turner says that we are "there," complacently observing that "the bulk of modern thought has simply dispensed with God."[80] Zimmer's argument was that we trust our symbols like "God" too much and though "symbols hold the mind to truth . . . [they] are not themselves the truth."[81]

GOD AND COGNITIVE MODESTY

Knowing how we know is the beginning of all wisdom. By knowledge we mean *awareness of reality.* The most common failings in epistemology (the study of how we know, of how we become aware of reality) are to *overestimate* our mental grasp and to *underestimate* the ways we grasp and become aware of reality. We totally comprehend nothing, but we go at our knowing in a rich diversity of ways. As knowers, we are both more versatile and less successful than we think. Figure 1 shows the complexities of knowing, from the simplicity of description to the subtlety of symbol.

Our simplest knowing is at the descriptive level where science tries to work.[82] (See the lower portion of the graph.) When we name something or someone at this level, we achieve some obvious success. To see a pencil and name it is an experience of accuracy—but not of comprehension, that is, we do not know everything about the pencil. If we take the reality of the pencil down to its atomic and subatomic levels, we are plunged into mystery that goes beyond our powers of description. When we recognize and name something a computer, we are also accurate, but the mystery is even greater, reaching such things as the unplumbable nature of electricity. When we name the person who owns the pencil or the

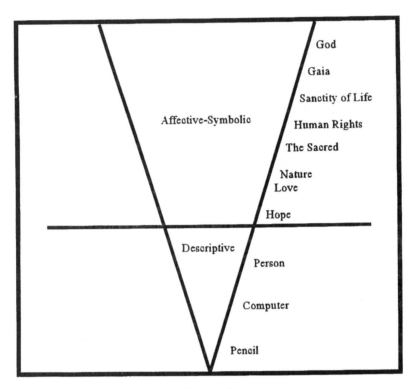

FIGURE 1
THE DIMENSIONS OF KNOWLEDGE

computer, and can distinguish this person from others, we are again seriously accurate, but the experience of what a person is and what makes people so valuable—an experience that happens to be the basis of all ethics and law—shows us to be, even more decidedly, unprofitable cognitive servants. The experience of "the sanctity of life" undergirds all national constitutions and legal systems and grounds all claims of human and civil "rights" and yet it remains ultimately beyond our powers of empirical analysis or description. We cannot explain empirically or rationally why the murder or abuse or enslavement of persons is a *desecration* or why it makes heroic sense to suffer and even to die for person-related causes. Civilization depends utterly on this knowledge but we are humbled by the question of how we know this knowledge. This dimension of our cognitive experience moves us to the upper level of the graph, the affective-symbolic level.[83]

At this level, where the most important knowing takes place, the kind of knowing that makes civil existence possible, cognition is more like touch than *vision*.[84] There is a veil between us and the reality. What we know is beyond the reach of tidy description, and yet we definitely do know. All knowledge, again, is awareness, and at this level of knowing our affections become the main medium of awareness. We feel more than we can say. Lovers understand this well. Rationalists are more obtuse. But this affection-fueled and affection-formed knowledge that will save the world if saved it will be—this knowledge that is the grounds of all ethics, law, and politics—is, in the terms of my graph, upper level knowledge. Unfortunately in our technicalized world, we are mesmerized by technical intelligence. We even imagine that machines (computers) have it and that the computer could be *Time*'s Man of the Year. Our public epistemology is dominated by rationalists and technologists and mechanistic conceptions of thought. Science and philosophy, alienated from their mystical personal roots—and to that degree dehumanized—need infusions of poetry, contemplation, and ethics. Phrased differently, they need respect for feeling and its elemental genius.

Again, with reference to the graph, at the upper level of knowing, the mind summons symbols, metaphors, images, poetry, and art to its purposes. When we speak of "nature," or "hope," or "human rights," or "souls," or "love," or "the sacred," or the "sanctity of life," or "ecology," "mother nature," "Gaia," or "God"—we are no longer naming individual things or people. We have departed from *things-ville*. We have moved beyond the comparatively paltry but decent and essential work of identifying pencils, computers, or discrete persons. We have moved to a confrontation with the ultimate challenge to language and thought. At this level, the mind is on safari, with tidy descriptive language left behind in the village of simplicities. Here conative intelligence struggles with our most important understandings, with experiences of truth that do not compute or fit onto a machine. These are not valley, but "peak experiences," or mystical moments, seeking—never with complete success— incarnation in symbol and poetry.

Sartre worried about our pernicious ability to make abstract that which is concrete, and he was right. Abstractions like "national security," "profitability," "progress," and "development" often leave out people and the rest of nature. *But we are equally prone to err by making concrete, that which is abstract and beyond our tidy picturing ability.* We try to treat the understandings of the upper, affective-symbolic level with the concreteness allowed by the lower, empirically descriptive level. We mistake Gods for pencils.

THE EXPERIENCE OF THE SACRED

The slightest reflection shows that we do experience *sacredness.* "The sanctity of life" is a meaningful term to theists and nontheists alike. The sacred is the name we give to what we find ineffably and uncompromisingly valuable. We also experience its opposite, profanation, when the sacred is offended and we reach for terms like "crime" or "atrocity" or "desecration" to describe it. Note the high emotive content of all these words. Emotive cognitive affectivity is the birthplace of the sacred. When sacred, person-related causes are imperiled, we appreciate the appropriateness of even dying for them and we call such sacrifice "supreme." So, again, sacrality is a fact of human life and there is no one who finds nothing sacred. We may and do call the wrong things sacred but we are inveterately *homo sacralis.* Religion, in this broad sense of a *response to the sacred* and religion in its various institutionalized forms, is and will be a major player in the planetary crisis . . . *for good or for ill.* Either you deal honestly with sacrality or you allow misplaced sacreds to achieve untested and unsuspected hegemony. Gods in secular or scientific dress are Gods all the same. Secularists who claim an a-religious chastity are promiscuous sacralizers under the covers of their alleged neutrality. Secularists who think the concept of religion or the sacred beneath them do understand power. And since religion, the experience of the sacred, is power, they do indeed go for it, but in sneaky and intellectually careless ways.

ETHICS AS RELIGIOUS

Religion and ethics are coextensive. The term "religious ethics" is a tautology, since *the sacred is the nucleus of the good* and there will be no solution to our crises unless that dynamic nucleus is touched. Motivation is that which turns the will on. "Values" is the name we give to will-stirring perceptions of the good. Values stir us. And values with a sacral core, moral values, can turn us on end. For that reason, sacrality must be front and center in modern discourse given the state of the world and its needs. Theistic religions can be more effective in modern discourse if they could become more modest. They may also find they have more to learn from nontheistic religions than they have dared to imagine.

GOD AS ADJECTIVE?

On the way to that needed modesty, theistic religions need to find better answers to the objection that their God(s) is an idol, an undue concretization of the sacred. They must face the *possibility* that God is an adjective, not a noun. The *sacred* and *Godliness* may best be seen as a dimension of our life experience, a way of describing the mysterious preciousness that fills our natural ambience. Sacrality in this understanding cannot be reduced or concretized in a cause, a person, a God, or in multiple Gods. It cannot be shrunken to the way we understand a pencil or even a friend. To do so is to slip from the difficult but rich affective-symbolic level of knowing to the simpler descriptive level. More seriously from the viewpoint of ecology, to project the experience of the sacred onto an immaterial God is to shortchange sacredness as a dimension of material life and turn it into an object of worship that is beyond our world and thus alien to life. Sacrality hypostatized (or reified) can easily be sacrality lost. The sacred as noun can take away the sacred as adjective. And with that modifier gone the modified is weakened; the sacred life mystery is not sacred anymore. Real sacredness is elsewhere—in heaven maybe.

A sense of the sacred is the soul of a healthy biophilia, but when sacredness is projected away into an otherworldly world its integral place in the experience of the miracle called *nature* is lost.

Many of the cosmogonic myths that still frame Western religious discourse today carried this logic all the way to hostility between the biological order and the divine.[85] The way to God was through denial of the body and the earth. Sanctity was *fuga mundi*, flight from the world. That is bad news for the world.

THE QUEST FOR THE MANUFACTURER

There are other reasons why theism is attractive to *homo faber*. When we look at the earth, which is a stunning mystery unfolding in the eternal mystery of the universe, a *homo faber* wants a maker. The "Who-done-it?" question is our customary way of *making sense of things*, and make sense we must for chaos is a horror. Sense-making *homo faber* knows that since somebody made the chair, somebody must similarly have made the strawberry, the DNA, and the universe.[86] Concluding to an almighty creator and provider God (while not explaining the imperfections and violence of nature) does enjoy a certain simplicity, but this gain is expensive. It proffers a kind of mechanistic simplicity that undercuts wonder. Inferring to a God is a problem solver, the aboriginal *deus ex machina*: the contemplative pause for wonder is a very different mission.

In theism, The *who-done-it?* question and *the sensemaker* in us conspire with the *false concretizer of the sacred* in us to reduce the experience of the sacred to the level of an individual entity, or more often, since monotheism is hard to cling to consistently, multiple individual entities. The God-concept both embodies the concept of the sacred and answers the manufacturing question. Theism, thus, is multifunctional and an understandable draw.

Fleeing the mystery of our existence by localizing and falsely concretizing the sacred and thus explaining our world is an old habit for the species. Arnold Toynbee traces out three stages of religious development, all showing the tendency to simplify the experience of sacrality by localizing it somewhere. Through most of history he contended, humans worshiped nature, and the Gods of this period were nature-Gods. When they began to conquer some of the forces of nature, they began to subordinate "the worship of conquered Nature to the worship of the collective human power that had given us our victory."[87] Our nations became our Gods. Enlil, the wind-God, became the deification of the state of Nippur. Nanna, the moon-God, did the same for Ur; as did Athena, the olive-Goddess, for Athens; Poseidon, the water-God for Corinth; and so forth. The third stage of religious history began with religions such as prophetic Judaism and Zoroastrianism. These religions moved away from the worship of nature Gods *and* from the devastating second stage, the worship of our national collectivities. This third stage was an attempt to locate the "ultimate spiritual reality" beyond the visible world.[88] This normally took the form of theism.[89]

As I see it, Toynbee's third stage still continued the localization of the sacred, but in a more symbolic, idealized, and Platonic form. Another stage may await us. The fourth stage would be to recognize the third stage as a more refined mistake, a more ethereal localization or concretization of the sacred. The monotheism of the third stage did tidy up Olympus and provide us with a single *Deus Faber* who replaced both the nature Gods and the nation Gods. Whatever new problems it presented, this was solid progress since the second stage divinization and worship of the state, which lives on today in the passions of nationalism, is totalitarian by implication. The "higher religions" gave us grounds to resist the claims of *Divus Caesar* by appeals to a higher, invisible authority. The prophets of Israel brilliantly illustrated this liberation. I must and do concede that there are many other ways in which a personalized God image can be valuable and has been a frequent boon in human history. *Deus vult*, the "will of God" has proved itself one of the most powerful motivators in human history. When the ancient Hebrews decided that God is concerned with the poor and the powerless and wants us to be similarly compassionate, history turned a moral corner. It was nothing less than a major moral mutation in the evolution of culture. The Spirits and Gods of native religions were said to love the earth and wanted us to cherish it also. All of that has been positive and has powered some of the major moral and political reforms in human history.[90] Of course, the *Deus vult* stoked the Crusaders' zeal and Hitler's troops wore *Gott mit uns* on their buckles. No hypothesis is without problems.

In sum, in this new hypothesis, God-talk, which presumes an individualized and even personalized source of everything, moves upper-level knowing (affective-symbolic) to lower-level knowing (description of individual entities). The temptations toward this maneuver are great. The mind is less taxed and the fear of the unknown is eased. By this stratagem of apotheosis, the big picture is made to seem as clear as all our little pictures and all our "Who-done-its?" are answered in one theistic swoop. The problem is that it might be too cheap a fix. It might put the mind at rest too quickly; problem-solving may replace mystery-immersion. And terrestrial life is mystery supreme.

If you posit reality as a problem rather than a mystery, you may solve the problem—-and stop, diverting your eyes from the mystery. Ratiocination may short-circuit contemplation. A superficial *figuring-it-out* may replace the ecstatic and wiser—but often disquieting—agony of wonder. And wonder, that hopeful peaking of the human spirit, is the last best hope of our planet and this precarious film on the face of the earth that we call life.

FAREWELL TO THEISM?

Theism, of course, will not melt away before the heat of my hypothesis. In its myriad forms it will be with us, we might say, forever. Alongside it will be the nontheistic and the many only vaguely theistic religions, and those religions for whom the idealized ancestors have more importance than a present but somewhat inconsequential God figure. The essential quality to bring peace to this melange is modesty. Modesty builds bridges. It even breeds a polite agnosticism about one's own conclusions. My God-questioning hypothesis takes aim at the unquestioning theism of the overly confident Abrahamic religions of Judaism, Christianity, and Islam. God is after all a hypothesis, a fallible inference. Monotheism is not based on irrefragable evidence but on surmise and assumption. Monotheists for whom nothing else makes sense could still be modest and learn to respect the religious spirit of those whose response to the sacred in our midst, to the sanctity of life, is sincere and even heroic . . . but not theistic. The non-theistic may be more reverent of the mystery of life.

Attention to our common moral ground builds bridges and is ultimately more practical than debating the existence of a distinct God. To that common moral ground I will return in a moment.

PRIMARY VERSUS REFLECTED VALUE

I have conceded that historical theism brought gains and still has motivating power; it also imports losses. If all the value that we see on this fair earth is secondary, a mere reflection of its hidden divine source, then we and the world are but a dim mirror of the real thing. Biocentricity gives way to theocentricity. Understandably, the "honor of God" may come to supersede not only earth, but "humanity" as Calvin insisted. If, on top of that, our true life is after death in union with this true and unreflected embodiment of value, then, once again, *fuga mundi*, the flight from the world taught by many religions makes sense. Earth as main stage becomes earth as prelude: the biological may be seen as hostile to the spiritual. At the least, its status is diminished. It is not our home but the proving ground for our real home beyond. That is troubling news for the rest of nature.

SACRAMENTALITY AS DEFENSE

Monotheism could mount a defense by saying that the God-image enhances our ecological concern by portraying nature as a sacrament or reflection of the creator God. Sacramentality could be a kind of reenchantment. It could bring the spirits back to the brooks and trees when these earthly realities are seen as reflections of the Great Spirit and Creator God. The sacramental vision could see the world as charged with the glory of God, dignified in its every aspect by the primordial Beauty it reflects.

But that sacramental view does not fit well with the facts of life.

Nature is not always nice. There is a lot to hate in nature. If nature is a sacramental portrait of a single divine author, that author has a split and often violent personality. It would be hard to explain to the rabbit being devoured by the wolf—or to the salmon rushing to spawn and becoming instead the bear's supper—that all of this reflects the tender mercies of a good God.[91] Indeed, both salmon and rabbit and victims of earthquakes and tornadoes would be more impressed by a dualistic, Manichaean theology which would posit two Gods, one good and one God-awful. By the philosophical principle *nil in effectu nisi in causa* (nothing is in the effect that is not in some way in the cause) the hateful things in nature—Ebola and AIDS viruses, childhood cancer, and other genetic and terrestrial disasters—could quite plausibly reflect the evil principle, the bad God. In this sense two Gods may make more sense than one. The route to reenchantment by way of sacramentality is a rough road to travel. A theodicy that would defend the honor of a single good God has never succeeded. The life that is good also bears the mark of the tragic. Violence is as natural as sunsets and roses. The sacramental view of nature and its theodicy must choke on that.

GOD-MADE MALE

Symbols are polyvalent. In some ways they inspire and in other ways they may wound. When "God" becomes incarnate and takes on gender and a place in history, the God-problems proliferate. Christian theologians have said that the incarnation of the male Jesus, as the preexistent second person of the trinity, sanctifies all of nature. But what does this say about nature if it needed such dramatic validation? And what dignity was nature missing the day before the first Christmas? And why a male? Arguably, the human male between fourteen and forty years of age is the most dangerous animal on this planet. Every day, whether we call them the IRA, Hamas, or simply terrorists, killers of this age group are at it. When speaking of the killing being done by Irish, Serbs, Rwandans, Ethiopians, or criminals everywhere, we are not referring to women and children. We are talking almost always about males between fourteen and forty. (Older males are in management, plotting these ventures.) Is the masculine incarnation of sacrality in Nicaean and Chalcedonic terms a symbol for all seasons? Was not the *de facto* Catholic elevation of Mary and many women saints to unofficial divinity not a correction of masculinist theology by popular religious imagination? And was this feminizing corrective not a tilt toward gentleness, both social and ecological? Indeed, is not popular religious imagination (called the *sensus fidelium* in Catholic theology) always more creative and more daringly poetic than academic theology? It is sometimes deviant, but then so too is academic theology, and it is hard to know which is ahead on the deviancy scale. At any rate, the New Testament is ambiguous on the divinity or preexistence of Jesus and offers scant consolation to later conciliar Christologies. Nonfeminist Christian theology is still in default in assessing the impact of this apotheosis of the masculine on the traditional disempowerment of women in the West.

Here again, we might ask: Is the exodus from the churches a loss of faith or a rebirth of the sense of the sacred, an inchoate religious renaissance in search of a new religious modality, a more meaningful religious poetry? "How many centuries is it," asked André Malraux, "since a great religion shook the world?"[92] We may already be rocking on the tremors of such a quake, such a birth of the sense of the sacred while hardly taking note of it.[93] The sense of the sacred may be more vibrant in the movements of ecofeminism, transnational human rights and peace activism, and the green revolution than in the traditionally assigned places.[94] The experience of that which is most precious in life (the sacred) may be fleeing decadence and seeking a more congenial home.

"POSTHUMOUS EGOISM"

In 1923 Charlotte Perkins Gilman suggested that for men death is the pivotal experience due to their hunting and warring past; for women, it is birth. The result is men's need for immortality, "a posthumous egoism, a demand for an eternal extension of personality" that amounts to "a limitless individualism."[95] Anne Wilson Schaef, a psychotherapist offering an empirical observation, says that women tend to "realize that immortality is not a genuine possibility and spend little or no time worrying about it."[96] Burying our dead in steel coffins, says Rosemary Radford Ruether is "a fundamental refusal to accept earth as our home and the plants and animals of earth as our kindred."[97] As I have already suggested, afterlife might do more than opiate the social conscience with hope for the sweet by and by. It can make our earth-life the prologue, not the text and context of our being. It can deterrestrialize our identity. It can make us strangers in this paradise, and estrangement is the gateway to enmity. If we have a claim on an afterlife, and the plants and the animals do not, we are not their kith and kin, nor do we share

their perils. *Earth as prolegomenon* and *earth as destiny* are
the ultimate in divergent worldviews and divergent ethics.

PROSPECTS

Religion, as a sense of the sacred, is needed to fuel the
necessary cultural revolutions to solve our planet's ills. As
André Malraux says, the twenty-first century will be spiritual
or it will not *be*. At the same time, the long-tenured explanation of the religiosacred is rejected by many of those in the
West who are most attuned to the earth-crisis . . . and who are
therefore by my definition quite religious. What greater challenge faces the modern servants of human imagination?

The search for meaning is an eternal passion. As Rubem
Alves says, we have a need "as powerful as sex and hunger:
the need to live in a world that makes sense."[98] Theism may
represent just one form of sense-making. Perhaps theists and
nontheists could unite in the recognition that they are both
meaning-searchers driven by the hope that the world is
marked more by *cosmos* than by *chaos*, more by *beauty* than
by *ugliness*. And despite the plethora of human and natural
miseries, there is a great wealth of cosmos and beauty.
Whether the cause of this is Nature or God is an issue beyond
all settling. And it is a mischievous issue if it distracts us
from the ecstasy our setting merits. Perhaps shared appreciation of the beauty and the cosmos of earth could heal our
multiple apartheids and bind us in a healthy solidarity. God-
talk that divides—overly confident God-talk—is better
unspoken.

Poetry elevated to the level of religion is the imperfect
best in human sense-making. Unfortunately, much of the
Western theological trade is plied in cultures that are poeti-
cally pallid. Remember Reinhold Niebuhr's lament: "How
can any age which is so devoid of poetic imagination as ours
be truly religious?"[99] Perhaps we are not up to the challenge
of cleansing our symbols and creating a new and unifying
religious poetry for a new age. So, is my final word a wail of
despair? No.

Maybe what Yeats wrote of the arts is true of religious thinkers. "The arts are at their best," he said, "when they are busy with battles that can never be won."[100] There is still that renewable and remarkable moral energy buried within the fossils of traditional religious symbol systems and reformers are at work on this, as I mentioned above. There is "theopolitical dynamite" buried in the scrolls and stories of the world's traditional religious poetry (the term is Pinchas Lapide's).[101]

But, a second hopeful front is opening. It involves discovering the *moral common ground* of the world's classical religions. Scholars have too often missed the moral commons on which all great religions meet. All religions have a common origin. Its names are awe, reverence, appreciation, wonder, and a sense of giftedness. To illustrate this, draw a line, mark its center point, and the world's religions all rise like radii from that same point. I call it "point wow!" It is the mystical moral core of all true religion. It is illustrated in Figure 2.

Alongside the horrors of the world, we see the first smiles of infants; the undefeatable growth of greenery from volcanic ash; the beauty of heroic love, of minds, and sunsets, mallards and the rose—and we say "Wow!" However undignified the epithet, this "Wow!" is the touchstone of civilization. This primal awe is the birth-zone of morality and religion. It is the foundational moral and religious experience.[102] The moral response pronounces the gift good; the religious response proclaims it holy and sacred.

From this point the radii—the world's religions, those of the past and those now aborning—take off on their symbolic journey through time, symbolizing and poetizing all the way. Some are theistic, some are not. They appear more diverse the further they go out into time, but bring them back to their starting point and you have the common ground of *humanitas* and religion.[103] Humanitarian agnosticism fits on this graph of religions when it too has its roots in the great awe that breeds the great oughts.[104] Those who call themselves atheists or agnostics may have more of a sense of the

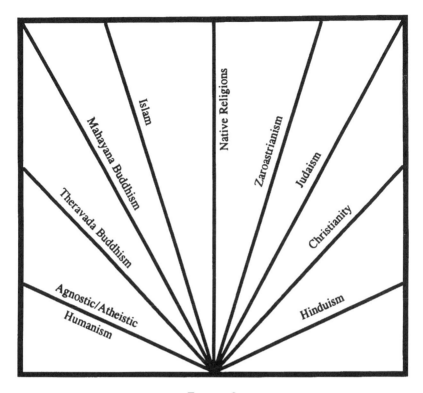

FIGURE 2
MODEL OF RELIGIONS

From Daniel C. Maguire, *The Moral Core of Judaism and Christianity* (Fortress Press, 1993), 41.

sacred than do initiates of "religions" grown cold. The mission of each of the "radii" is to converse, not to convert, and to rebaptize their symbols regularly in their originating awe, rejecting some, redoing others to make them more worthy of their origins. Religions that meet on their moral commons— maintaining mutual respect for their varying dogmas and poetries—hold great hope for the earth and our future on it.

Religions in their institutionalized forms are cumbersome and full of contradictions. They can both change cultures and get trapped in worn-out cultures. They can promote revolution or enshrine archaism. But historically they have been the vehicle for ideals that can affect, shape, and creatively undermine cultures. They cannot be left out as the human race rethinks its future on this seriously damaged planet where Extinction threatens to become the Earth God.

And religion in the general sense, as the experience of sacredness, is at the core of ecological ethics and human rights thinking. The sense of the sacred energizes and drives ethical inquiry. We have to redo humanity to survive. If current trends continue, we will not. Cleverness will not save us. Cleverness has brought us to our knees. Wisdom is our need and the heart of wisdom is awe. Ethics is awe's strategy.

Economics, political science, and sociology began as subsets of ethics. They quickly left home in search of a chimerical "value-free objectivity." They thus divorced themselves from awe's strategy. Their original purpose was to plan a just and livable society and to chart the meanings of our "common good." But now those runaways jog over ground waters that will poison their children, under skies of depleting ozone. Ethics and its undergirding awe can only be neglected for a time. Ethics after all is the art-science of life and life will not long be mocked by those who would substitute unfeeling technique for the passions and sensitivities of wisdom.

CONCLUSION

One tragic truth has become clear. For much of the world it is already too late. It is apocalypse now. The neurological and physical damage of many caught in the quiet holocaust of hunger is beyond repair. In 1990 the World Bank estimated the number of those in absolute poverty—those who lack the basic necessities of life—at 1.1 billion.[105] Others say it could be as high as 2 billion people.[106] Our destruction of the earth and its children is well on. Some land, like that of Haiti and Ethiopia, seems permanently spoiled. Yet, despair is the ultimate ethical apostasy. Ethics is the progeny of hope.

There are, in fact, glimmerings of hope. An African woman declared at the United Nations conference in Cairo: "I have never yet met people who do not want to help themselves." The feeble mind of humankind is coming into some dim focus. Green ideas are birthing, even in technopolis. And in Cairo in 1994, for the first time in history, the human race sat in international assembly *with women as well represented as men* and did ethics on the earth's future. We felt there a surge of hope transfusing into the human bloodstream.

RISING FOR THE SANCTUS

Robin Morgan wrote the poem for our times called "Peony." The peony begins encased in thick green rind. Its explosion of beauty can only be released if small herbivorous ants nibble at it for weeks. As Morgan puts it, "the bloom cannot unfist itself" without them. Then the miracle happens. "This frozen explosion of petals,/abristle with extremist beauty,/like an entire bouquet on a single stem,/or a full chorus creamy-robe rippling/to its feet for the *sanctus*."/She then compares the work of the tediously nibbling ants to that of all those who work to save the earth. "Each of us nibbling discreetly/to release the flower/. . . sometimes astonished by a glimpse/. . . at how many of us there are."/She concludes celebrating all "who are still here, who dare,/tenacious, to nibble toward such blossoming/of this green stubborn bud/some call a world."[107]

With the permission of the gentle poet, this hope-stirring poem in its symphonic fullness follows.

Peony
by Robin Morgan

What appears to be
this frozen explosion of petals
abristle with extremist beauty
like an entire bouquet on a single stem
or a full chorus creamy-robed rippling
to its feet for the sanctus
is after all a flower,

perishable, with a peculiar
history. Each peony
blossoms only after
the waxy casing thick around
its tight green bud is eaten literally
away by certain small herbivorous ants
who swarm round the stubborn rind
and nibble gently for weeks to release
the implosion called a flower. If
the tiny coral-colored ants have been
destroyed, the bloom cannot unfist itself
no matter how carefully forced to umbrage
by the finest hothouse gardeners.

Unrecognized, how recognizable:

Each of us nibbling discreetly
to release the flower,
usually not even knowing
the purpose—only the hunger;

each mostly unaware of any others,
sometimes surprised by a neighbor,
sometimes (so rarely) astonished
by as glimpse into one corner
at how many of us there are;

enough to cling at least, swarm back
remain, whenever we're shaken
off or drenched away
by the well-meaning gardener, ignorant
as we are of our mission, of our being
equal in and to the task.

Unequal to the task: a word
like "revolution," to describe
what our drudge-cheerful midwifery
will bring to bear—with us not here
to see it, satiated, long since
rinsed away, the job complete.

Why then do I feel this tremble,
more like a contraction's aftermath
release, relax, relief
than like an earthquake; more
like a rustling in the belly,
or the resonance a song might make
en route from brain to larynx,
> *as if now, here, unleaving itself of all*
> *old and unnecessary outer layers*

>> *butterfly from chrysalis*
>> *snake from cast skin*
>> *crustacean from shell*
>> *baby from placenta*

something alive before
only in Anywoman's dreamings
begins to stretch, arch, unfold
each vein on each transparency opening proud,
unique, unduplicate,
each petal stiff with tenderness,
each gauzy wing a different shading flecked
ivory silver tangerine moon cinnamon amber flame
hosannas of lucidity and love in a wild riot,
a confusion of boisterous order
all fragrance, laughter, tousled celebration—
> *only a fading streak like blood*
> *at the center, to remind us we were there once*

>> *but are still here, who dare,*
>> *tenacious, to nibble toward such blossoming*
>> *of this green stubborn bud*
>> *some call a world.*

NOTES

1. Janet Abramovitz, *Imperiled Waters, Impoverished Future: The Decline of Freshwater Ecosystems* (Washington, D.C.: Worldwatch Institute, 1996), 39–41. On the impact of demographic pres-

sure, land use policies, and "development" on the Chesapeake Bay, see *World Resources: 1994–95* (Baltimore: World Resources Institute, 1994), 39–41.)

2. Cited by Timothy E. Wirth, Under secretary of State for Global Affairs, at National Press Club, July 12, 1994.

3. See Paula DePerna, "Population, the Environment, and Human Potential," in *Conscience*, vol. XIV, no. 3, Autumn (1993), 4. DePerna is describing the devastation of Haiti's ecology.

4. Gretchen C. Daily, "Restoring Value to the World's Degraded Lands," *Science*, vol. 269, July 21, 1995, 351.

5. Population Reports, Series M, No. 10, Population Information Program, Johns Hopkins University, May 1992, 8, 16.

6. Lester R. Brown, *Who Will Feed China?: Wake-up Call for a Small Planet.* (New York: Norton, 1995), 30.

7. Walter Corson, Editor, *The Global Ecology Handbook* (Boston: Beacon Press, 1990), 68. See Noeleen Heyzer, *The Balancing Act: Population, Development, and Women in an Era of Globalization* (Chicago and New Delhi: A publication of The John D. And Catherine T. MacArthur Foundation, 1996), 16–17

8. Joel E. Cohen, "Population Growth and the Earth's Human Carrying Capacity," *Science*, vol. 269, July 21, 1995, 341.

9. See Anne E. Platt, *Infecting Ourselves: How Environmental and Social Disruptions Trigger Disease* (Washington, D.C.: Worldwatch Paper 129, 1996).

10. Faiza Rady, "More Food, Not More Cows," *Al-Ahram.* September 5, 1994, 8.

11. *Ibid.*

12. Walter H. Corson, *The Global Ecology Handbook*, 7.

13. Lester R. Brown, *Who Will Feed China?: Wake-up Call for a Small Planet* (New York: Norton, 1995), 30.

14. Gretchen C. Daily and Paul R. and Ann H. Ehrlich, "Food Security, Population and Environment," *Population and Development Review* 19, no. 1 (March 1993), 4.

15. Paul Kennedy, Preparing for the Twenty-First Century (New York: Vintage, 1994), 95.

16. See Paul Kennedy, *Preparing for the Twenty-first Century*, 96.

17. David Loy, "The Religion of Consumption," an unpublished paper written for a symposium of the Religious Consultation on Population, Reproductive Health and Ethics.

18. Alan Durning, *How Much Is Enough—The Consuming Society and the Future of the Earth* (New York: W. W. Norton & Co., 1992), 38.

19. Alan Durning, *How Much Is Enough?*, 51. Population, consumption, and ecology are interlocking elements of the earth crisis. An excellent study by multiple experts exploring the religious and economic dimensions of the crisis is Harold Coward, ed., *Population, Consumption, and the Environment: Religious and Secular Responses* (Albany: State University of New York Press, 1995).

20. The Bretton Woods agreement of July, 1994 assumed that the world was in Henry Morgenthau's words, "infinitely blessed with natural riches." For Morgenthau and those who joined him in fashioning the World Bank and the International Monetary Fund and laying the groundwork for the General Agreement on Tariffs and Trade—the economic axiom was "that prosperity has no fixed limits. It is not a finite substance to be diminished by division." The error here is psychotic in its distance from our physical and biological reality. David Korten, in a brilliant speech given in October 1994 to the Environmental Grantmakers Association at the very Bretton Woods site concluded: "The vision of Bretton Woods is an illusion; its failure of purpose was inevitable." Governmental concern for the poor and the environment and governmental recognition of Need as a basic human reality are replaced by corporate growth mania and greed. The logic of Bretton Woods and the institutions it spawned is such that large corporations now constitute "a global financial system that has become the world's most powerful governance institution." See David C. Korten, "Sustainability and the Global Economy: Beyond Bretton Woods," People-Centered Development Forum, 14 E. Seventeenth Street, Suite 5, New York, NY 10003. Phone: 212-620-7137; Fax: 212-242-1901.

21. *Population and Development: Programme of Action adopted at the International Conference on Population and Development, Cairo, 5–13, September 1994* (New York: United Nations Publications, Sales No. E.95. XIII.7, 1995), 12. See also 7.15.

22. *Ibid.*, 7.3 7.12.

23. *Ibid.*, 7.12

24. Sharon L. Camp, "Global Population Stabilization: A 'No Regrets' Strategy," in *Conscience*, 8.

25. Urbanization is credited as a major influence on reduced fertility. In 1981, for example, the total fertility rate in rural areas in China was 2.9 children per woman while it was 1.4 in urban areas. See Zeng Yi and James W. Vaupel, "The Impact of Urbanization and Delayed Childbearing on Population Growth and Aging in China," *Population and Development Review*, 15, no. 3 (September 1989), 425–45.

26. Paul Kennedy, *Preparing for the Twenty-First Century*, 167. In a study of ten years in Hebei Province, Jiali Li questions the effectiveness of the one-child policy especially for peasant women. Li does conclude that women with "worker registration" as opposed to "peasant registration" were more likely to adhere to the policy because of the serious loss of privileges they would incur. See Jiali Li, "China's One-Child Policy: How and How Well Has It Worked? A Case Study of Hebei Province, 1979–88," *Population and Development Review*, 21, no. 3 (September 1995), 563–85.

27. Griffith Feeney and Wang Feng, "Parity Progression and Birth Intervals in China: The Influence of Policy in Hastening Fertility Decline," in *Population and Development Review* 19, no. 1 (March 1993), 95.

28. Amartya Sen, "Population: Delusion and Reality," *The New York Review of Books*, September 22, 1994, 70.

29. Lester R. Brown, *Who Will Feed China*, 35. James A. Nash who has written wisely and carefully on the ethics of the earth allows for the limits of voluntarism, saying that "enforcement procedures ranging from bans to incentives" must be considered. "Human Rights and the Environment: New Challenge for Ethics," *Theology and Public Policy* 4, no. 2 (Fall 1992), 55.

30. Griffith Feeney and Wang Feng, "Parity Progression and Birth Intervals in China," 96.

31. In the West, it has been customary to impute every manner of evil to China's governmental policies, including a ratio-skewing increase in female infanticide. A study by a Chinese scholar faces the question of whether a resurgence of female infanticide is a major cause of the high reported sex ration at birth. Their answer is "negative." See Zeng Yi, Tu Ping, Gu Baochang, Xu Yi, Li Bohua, Li Yongping, "Causes and Implications of the Recent Increase in the Reported Sex Ratio at Birth in China," in China," in *Population and Development Review* 19, no. 2 (June 1993), 294.

32. Daniel C. Maguire, "Poverty, Population, and the Catholic Tradition," in *Religious and Ethical Perspectives on Population Issues*, published by the Religious Consultation on Population, Reproductive Health and Ethics, Washington, D.C., 15.

33. Luo Ping, "Reflections on My Impressions of Northern Europe" in *Reflections and Resonance: Stories of Chinese Women Involved in International Preparatory Activities for the 1995 NGO Forum on Women* (Beijing: The Ford Foundation, 1995), 203. Ping is critical of the Chinese practice of putting the burden for fertility control on women.

34. The word "ecology" normally refers only to our biological ecology. This betrays a materialistic bias since our *oikos*, the matrix of our lives, involves more than air, water, and soil. A holistic sense of ecology includes culture and the presence or absence of justice, hope, beauty, and joy. But the word is busy enough on its biological mission and we must leave it there.

35. The ethical definition of government is a neglected challenge in population discussions. All definitions of government contain a usually well-veiled worldview and theory of social justice. Minimalist definitions of government are the American vogue, beginning with Tom Paine's viewing government as a "necessary evil." Drawing from the Jewish *Sedaqah* tradition and the Christian social justice traditions government can be defined as *the prime protector of the common good with a special mandate to care for the poor and the powerless in society.* See Daniel C. Maguire, *The Moral Core of Judaism and Christianity* (Minneapolis: Fortress Press, 1993), 161–64.

36. Amartya Sen, "Population: Delusion and Reality," 70–71. Sen maintains a remarkable optimism in this article with an Enlightenment confidence in people doing good rationally. He is especially buoyed by recent gains in food production and the lowering of food prices. He properly sees that demographic and collegial decision-making processes, education of women as well as of men, good health care, security for the aged, and expansion of opportunity for decent jobs will bring fertility rates down. Apocalyptic doomsayers on population he accuses of "terrorizing" tactics. He neglects the apparent maximization of fishing capacities, the loss of topsoil, the drastic shortage of water regionally. He accents more the global good news over the regional tragedies. It would be hard to convince a hungry child in crowded Cairo or Calcutta that population is not a problem of apocalyptic proportions for them and that cheap food is available. Victims of desertification would be equally hard to console with global good news.

37. Bill McKibben, "The Enigma of Kerala," in *Utne* Reader, March–April, 1996, no. 74, 102–12.

38. Orville Schell, "China—The End of an Era," *The Nation*, Vol. 261, July 17/24, 1995, 94.

39. Thomas Aquinas, *Opera Omnia: Sententia Libri Politicorum* (Rome: Ad Sanctae Sabinae, 1971). Book II, Chap. 15; also, chap. 6, 13, 17.

40. Johannes Messner, *Social Ethics; Natural Law in the Western World* (St. Louis: Herder Book Co., 1964), 704–5, n. 1.

41. John Stuart Mill, *On Liberty* [1859] (Chicago: Encyclopedia Britannica Great Books, 1952), 3,191.

42. Again, I make reference to my defense of this definition of government in Daniel C. Maguire, *The Moral Core of Christianity and Judaism*, 161–64.

43. Azizah Y. al-Hibri, "Family Planning and Islamic Jurisprudence," in *Religious and Ethical Perspectives on Population Issues* (Washington, D.C.: The Religious Consultation on Population, Reproductive Health and Ethics, 1993), 6.

44. Homa Hoodfar, "Devices and Desires: Population Policy and Gender Roles in the Islamic Republic," in *Middle East Report*, vol. 190, September–October, 1994, 17.

45. Nikki R. Keddie, "The Rights of Women in Contemporary Islam," in Leroy S. Rouner, ed., *Human Rights and the World's Religions* (Notre Dame, Indiana: University of Notre Dame Press, 1988), 92.

46. Sally Ethelston, "Gender, Population, Environment," in *Middle East Report*, 3.

47. Harold Coward, "Is Population Pressure or Excess Consumption Destroying the Environment? Points of Consensus and Divergence in the Response of World Religions." Unpublished paper. See Harold Coward, *Population, Consumption, and the Environment: Religious and Secular Responses* (Albany: State University of New York Press), 1995.

48. *Ibid.*, 98–99.

49. See Harold Coward, *Population, Consumption, and the Environment: Religious and Secular Responses* (Albany: State University of New York Press), 1995. In this judicious and helpful *tour de force*, scholars such as Sharon Joseph Levy, Rita M. Gross, Daisy Sewid-Smith, Catherine Keller, Nawal Ammar, Klaus Klostermaier, Jordan Paper, and Li Chuang Paper explore and develop the neglected resources of aboriginal religions, Judaism, Christianity, Islam, Hinduism, Buddhism, and Chinese religions.

50. Douglas Johnston and Cynthia Sampson, Editors, *Religion, The Missing Dimension of Statecraft* (New York: Oxford University Press, 1994).

51. Wilfred Cantwell Smith, *The Faith of Other Men* (New York: Harper & Row, 1962), 127.

52. The State of the World's Children's: 1995 (New York: Oxford, 1995), 52.

53. Arnold Toynbee, *Study of History*, Abridgement by D. C. Somervell (New York: Oxford University Press, 1957, vol. 2), 98.

54. *Ibid.*, 98–99.

55. See Daniel C. Maguire, *The Moral Core of Judaism and Christianity* (Minneapolis: Fortress, 1993), 47–53 and Part Two: Scripting a New Humanity.

56. Elaine Pagels, *Adam, Eve, and the Serpent* (New York: Random House, 1988), xxiii–iv.

57. Garry Wills, "Faith and the Race for God and Country," *Sojourners* 15 (March 14, 1988), 4–5.

58. Daniel L. Pals, *Seven Theories of Religion* (New York: Oxford University Press, 1996), 9. Pals is referring to the work of E. B. Tylor, James Frazer, Sigmund Freud, Emile Durkheim, Karl Marx, Mircea Eliade, E. Evans-Prichard, and Clifford Geertz. He allows that this is only a sampling of those who have similar cultural impact.

59. Jack Miles, *God: A Biography* (New York: Alfred A. Knopf, 1995), 4.

60. Lynn White, "The Historical Roots of our Ecologic Crisis, *Science*, vol. 155 (March 10, 1967), 1203–07.

61. Daniel Pals, *Seven Theories of Religion*, 5.

62. Actually, as the group "Atheists for Niebuhr" concluded, it may be possible to have a great deal left even after removing the God imagery. Niebuhr was a thorough going theist. Prescinding from a theist's presuppositions about God might leave the substance of her or his thought intact. The theistic imagery might be translatable into other symbols. In my *The Moral Core of Judaism and Christianity* I wrote with the assumption that even the Jewish and Christian scriptures, theistically permeated as they are, can be understood nontheistically with profit.

63. In 1958 only one person in 25 had left his or her childhood church but by 1984 one in three had done so. See Robert Bellah et al. *The Good Society* (New York: Vintage, 1992), 324, n. 30.

64. M. Douglas Meeks, *God the Economist: The Doctrine of God and Political Economy* (Minneapolis: Fortress Press, 1989), 120.

65. *Calvini Opera* in *Corpus Reformatorum*, 8:476; 24:360; 44:346.

66. Wisdom, 8:1.

67. Loren Eiseley, *The Invisible Pyramid: A Naturalist Analyses the Rocket Century* (New York: Scribners, 1970), 143.

68. David Hume, *The Natural History of Religion*, H. E. Root, editor (Stanford: Stanford University Press, 1957 [1757]), 53. See Stewart Guthrie, *Faces in the Clouds: A New Theory of Religion* (New York: Oxford University Press, 1993), 21–22.

69. In a fascinating study, Mark William Worthing notes the increasing amount of God-talk among theoretical physicists. He finds that the result is often pantheistic or panentheistic or that God like a mathematical *x* is the name for the infinite unreachable horizon of our knowledge. With all this fascination with Godly talk, science does not pretend to prove or disprove the existence of such a Being. Mark William Worthing, *God, Creation, and Contemporary Physics* (Minneapolis: Fortress, 1996). Jewish and Christian theologies do by their hypotheses lure the scientists. As theologian Emil Brunner says, "The theological statement: God is the 'Creator of Heaven and earth,' brings this affirmation into the sphere of facts which are accessible to our natural knowledge," Emil Brunner, *The Christian Doctrine of Creation and Redemption* (Philadelphia: Westminster, 1952), 5. This doctrine assumes that God has to be part of the explanation of how things got to be what they are and how the world works. All of that assumes God as a component or active entity. This means that even mainstream creation theology which, unlike the fundamentalists, concedes the reality of evolution is "creation science" of a sort. Like the fundamentalists' "creation science" all creation theology addresses the scientific questions: How did it get started? and How does it work?

70. Theists themselves do not agree on the nature of their God or on the force of their arguments for the existence of this God. There are varying and contradictory images of God in the Bibles of Jews and Christians.

71. Augustine *Sermo* 52, c. 6, n. 16 (*Patres Latini*, 38, 360).

72. Thomas Aquinas, *Quaestio Disputata de Spiritualibus Creaturis* 11, ad. 3.

73. Thomas Aquinas, *Summa Theologiae*, I, q. 3. The idea that analogy comes to the rescue has enjoyed a long and hopeful tenure. That means that we cannot know God but we can know what God is like. However, analogy is only helpful as we move from the more obvious to the less obvious. It only works between comprehensi-

bles. You cannot say that God is incomprehensible and then bring analogy in to save the day and hide the logical contradiction.

74. Elizabeth A. Johnson, *She Who Is: The Mystery of God in Feminist Theological Discourse* (New York: Crossroad, 1993), 7, 109.

75. Sallie McFague, *Models of God: Theology for an Ecological, Nuclear Age* (Minneapolis: Fortress, 1987), 35.

76. Humphrey Palmer, *Analogy* (London: MacMillan, 1973), xv.

77. Ian Barbour, *Myths, Models, and Paradigms* (New York: Harper and Row, 1974), 19.

78. Gordon D. Kaufman, *The Theological Imagination: Constructing the Concept of God* (Philadelphia: Westminster Press, 1981).

79. Heinrich Zimmer, *Philosophies of India*, ed. Joseph Campbell (Princeton: Princeton University Press, 1951), 1, 13.

80. James Turner, *Without God. Without Creed: The Origins of Unbelief in America* (Baltimore: Johns Hopkins University Press), 1985, 222.

81. Zimmer, *Philosophies of India*, 2.

82. When science begins to ask with Carl Sagan, introducing Stephen Hawking "why nature is the way it is; where the cosmos came from or whether it was always here; if time will one day flow backward and effects precede causes . . . why we remember the past and not the future, . . ." and so on, we can see that science also is into the affective-symbolic probing phase of intelligence at the upper level of my graph. Stephen W. Hawking, *A Brief History of Time* (New York: Bantam Books, 1988), ix. For the movement of science into the realm thought to be reserved to theology, see Rosemary Radford Ruether, *Gaia and God* (San Francisco: Harper, 1994).

83. Interestingly, Thomas Aquinas speaking of faith (a way of knowing religious and moral truth) has a certitude that exists "*in genere affectionis*," in the realm of affection. He says that "the knowledge of faith proceeds from the will." *Commentum in Quatuor Libros Sententiarum Magistri Petri Lombardi*, Dist. 23, q.

2, a. 3, and Dist. 23, q. 2, a. 1. See also *Summa Theologiae* II IIq. 45, a. 2 where affective knowing is described. In terms of my model this supports the idea that cognition of moral values and matters of the sacred are animated by affectivity and are in a cognitive class distinct from descriptive knowledge of empirical realities.

84. See Daniel C. Maguire, *The Moral Choice* (Winston: Harper & Row, 1979), Chapter Three, "The Meaning of Morals," 58–105; Daniel C. Maguire and A. Nicholas Fargnoli, *On Moral Grounds* (New York: Crossroad, 1991), 19–25; Daniel C. Maguire, *The Moral Revolution* (San Francisco: Harper & Row, 1986), "The Knowing Heart and the Intellectualistic Fallacy," 254–70.

85. See Rosemary Radford Ruether, *Gaia and God* (San Francisco: Harper, 1992), Chapters One and Two.

86. See Stewart Guthrie, *Faces in the Clouds: A New Theory of Religion* (New York: Oxford University Press, 1993). Guthrie's theory is that religion is a manifestation of our innate penchant to make sense of our setting by anthropomorphism.

87. Arnold J. Toynbee, *Change and Habit: The Challenge of Our Time* (New York: Oxford University Press, 1966), 26.

88. *Ibid.*, 106–7.

89. Guthrie argues that even Buddhism which in its more philosophical formulations denies a God figure, makes Buddha into a very identifiable God. *Faces in the Clouds*, 19.

90. My book, *The Moral Core of Judaism and Christianity* (Minneapolis: Fortress, 1993), explores the perennially renewable moral energies of two of the world's traditional religions, Judaism and Christianity, and credits them with major salutary reforms in human history . . . reforms that could be replicated to meet modern problems. It does this while acknowledging their historical debits.

91. James Nash says that Genesis can be accused of both "moral insensitivity" and "romanticism" in presenting nature as "good" and, even "very good." *Loving Nature* (Nashville: Abingdon, 1991), 98. Nature that is "red in tooth and claw" and strikes us down with cruel malignancies and sadistic viruses deserves more chastened and balanced admiration. There is a lot to despise in nature.

92. André Malraux, *Anti-Memoirs*, tr. by Terence Kilmartin (New York: Holt, 1968), 2.

93. See Jeremy Rifkin, *Biosphere Politics: A New Consciousness for a New Society* (New York: Crown Publishers, 1991).

94. On the feminist reforms of the world's institutionalized religions see P. Cooey, W. Eakin, and J. McDaniel, *After Patriarchy: Feminist Transformations of the World Religions* (Maryknoll, New York: Orbis Books, 1991).

95. Charlotte Perkins Gilman, *His Religion and Hers* (New York: Century, 1923), 46–47.

96. Anne Wilson Schaef, *Women's Reality: An Emerging Female System in the White Male Society* (Minneapolis: Winston Press, 1981), 142.

97. Rosemary Radford Ruether, *Sexism and God-Talk: Toward a Feminist Theology* (Boston: Beacon Press, 1983), 258.

98. Rubem Alves, *What Is Religion?* (Maryknoll, New York: Orbis Books, 1984), 21.

99. Reinhold Niebuhr, *Leaves from the Notebooks of a Tamed Cynic* (New York: Harper & Row, 1957), 167.

100. Frank Tuohy, *Yeats* (New York: New Amsterdam, 1976), 9.

101. Pinchas Lapide, *The Sermon on the Mount: Utopia or Program for Action* (Maryknoll, New York: Orbis Books, 1986), 29.

102. In my *The Moral Choice* (Garden City, N.Y.: Doubleday, 1978; Minneapolis: Winston Press, 1979), Chapter Three, and again in Daniel C. Maguire and A. Nicholas Fargnoli, *On Moral Grounds: The Art/Science of Ethics* (New York: Crossroad, 1991) Part One, I discuss the foundational moral experience. In my *The Moral Core of Judaism and Christianity*, I argue that the religious and moral foundational experiences are one.

103. The quest for a common moral ground (and deriving from that a common legal, juridical, and political ground) is a recurrent theme in Western literature. Cicero insisted that there should not be one law for Rome and another for Athens, neither should law in its essence be changed. Rather he saw "una lex" for "omnes gentes

et omni tempore." One eternal law for all nations. Seneca also spoke of a shared law for the entire human race . . . "commune jus generis humani." Dante later saw the human race as enjoying an essential unity . . . "totum humanum genus ordinatur ad unum." Francisco de Vitoria saw the whole world as somehow one nation . . . "totus orbis aliquo modo est una res publica." Kant and other philosophers would reflect this desire for one "Weltrepublik." See Georgio del Vecchio, *Man and Nature* (Notre Dame, Indiana: University of Notre Dame Press, 1969), 27.

104. Helpful efforts to explore the common moral grounds of world religions, are Leroy S. Rouner, Ed., *Human Rights and the Worlds' Religions* (Notre Dame, Indiana: University of Notre Dame Press, 1988) and Arlene Swidler, ed., *Human Rights in Religious Traditions* (New York: The Pilgrim Press, 1982); David Hallman, ed., *Ecotheology: Voices from South and North* (Maryknoll, N.Y.: Orbis Books, 1994).

105. The World Bank, *World Development Report 1990* (New York: Oxford University Press, 1990), 28.

106. H. Jeffrey Leonard and Montague Yudelman, *Environment and the Poor: Development Strategies for a Common Agenda* (New Brunswick: Transaction Books, 1989), 9–10.

107. "Peony" from *Upstairs in the Garden: Poems Selected and New, 1968–1988* by Robin Morgan. Copyright (c) 1990 by Robin Morgan. By permission. New York: Norton, 1990.

Introduction to Next Journey

LARRY L. RASMUSSEN

Working from population and consumption issues in a male-and rich-dominated world as these were exposed to the sun at the historic Cairo meeting, these pages have moved thus far from a profile of earth's distress into the moral framework needed to address these woes. Changes of the kind and scale needed, requiring men to share real power with women and the rich to share real power with the poor, will not happen without something that reaches to the depth of conviction, power, and ardor of religion. Thus the shared human experience of the sacred offers a foundation for the pursuit together of the common good. This sense of the sacred—Luther's "awe and reverence in the face of life"—is the nucleus of the good and the grounding of the moral framework presented to this point.

Assuming this framework and with a view to the pressing issues exposed and debated in Cairo and around the world, we now go on to scan the long history that brought us thus far on the way, a history that, whatever its manifold complexity, has been male-led and dominated by European and "neo-European" forces. With that history on the table, as well as the moral framework supplied above, the question becomes this: What specific moral norms and what kind of policy can guide sustainable communities and genuinely shared power? With these offerings the book closes and invites the reader's own energies and imagination for the work ahead.

NEXT JOURNEY:
SUSTAINABILITY FOR SIX BILLION AND MORE

LARRY L. RASMUSSEN

"Sustainability" is the capacity of natural and social systems to survive and thrive together indefinitely. "Population" is the bland synonym we currently use for earth's most exuberant species. "Development" is the post–World War II description of socioeconomic progress on the model of industrialized nations. Sustainability, population, development— these are the key elements of humankind's next journey. Reflection on the reality they inhabit, and what it means for living, structures this essay.

The defining global gatherings of the United Nations conferences in Rio (Environment and Development, 1992), Vienna (Human Rights, 1993), Cairo (Population and Development, 1994), Copenhagen (Social Development, 1995), Beijing (Fourth World Conference on Women, 1995), and Istanbul (Habitat II, 1996) are the sources of present preoccupation with sustainability, population, and development. But the reality they pose for earth community's next journey has a very long history, around two enduring issues: (1) How humans live in a sustainable relationship with the rest of earth; and (2) how we live with the play of human power, both in human-human configurations (the nature of society) and in human-biosphere configurations (society in nature). This long history and where it has now deposited us, especially in its Western-and male-led phase of globalization, is the initial undertaking. Policy orientation follows from the historical narrative.

SWEET BETSY AND HER AVALANCHE

The New York Times Book Review ran a piece entitled "Developing Ourselves to Death." It briefly investigates Bruce Rich's *Mortgaging the Earth: The World Bank, Environmental Impoverishment, and the Crisis of Development.* The reviewer opens with this: "Economic development may seem so much a part of modern times as to render self-evident Bruce Rich's premise that it 'is now the organizing principle for almost every society and nation on the planet.'"[1] Yet Rich notes that it is "a relatively new idea in history, spreading from western Europe in the seventeenth century to conquer the world over the next three centuries."[2] Then Stevens, the reviewer, says, "These are the same three centuries in which people have most extensively altered the global environment."[3] *Mortgaging the Earth* goes on from here. It does not pursue the relatively recent domination of economic development or the linkages suggested by the juxtaposition of economic development and environmental transformation. Rather, it investigates the policies of the World Bank as an agent of destructive modern development.

But what about those linkages, and the currents this "relatively new idea in history" of economic development set in motion? What connections are there, for example, when the following three citations by four famous authors in three famous books are laid side-by-side? Or are the ties ephemeral, wisps of smoke accidentally crossing the same sky?

The first is from Adam Smith in *Wealth of Nations.* Writing in the precocious year of 1776, Smith said, apparently with some confidence: "The discovery of America, and that of a passage to the East Indies by the Cape of Good Hope, are the two greatest and most important events recorded in the history of mankind."[4] Little more than a half century later, Charles Darwin, in *The Voyage of the Beagle* (1839), noted that "[w]herever the European had trod, death seems to pursue the aboriginal. We may look to the wide extent of the Americas, Polynesia, the Cape of Good Hope, and Australia, and we find the same result." And only nine years after Darwin, in 1848, Karl Marx and Friedrich Engels included this in the *Manifesto of the Communist Party*: "The discovery of America, [and] the rounding of the Cape opened up fresh ground for the rising bourgeoisie. The East Indian and Chinese markets, the colonization of America, trade with the colonies, the increase in the means of exchange and in commodities generally, gave to commerce, to navigation, to industry an impulse never before known, and thereby, to the revolutionary element in the tottering feudal society, a rapid development."[5]

Intriguing, is it not, that a moral philosopher tracking early capitalist economies, a biologist describing natural selection and developing evolution as a theory, and social historians and critics of industrial capitalism, none of whom is reading the other, should all mention the discovery of America and the rounding of the Cape of Good Hope as epoch-making events? But more intriguing are the possible historical connections of the "most important events recorded in the history of mankind" (Smith) to the revolutionary change and development of European society (Marx and Engels) and both of these to the death of aboriginal peoples around the world (Darwin). And all this recorded, not in 1992 with a gaze back over five hundred tumultuous years on the occasion of the rediscovery of Columbus by America, but independently of one another within three quarters of a century beginning with 1776!

These three citations (the fourth is set aside for a moment) are the frontispiece of Alfred Crosby's *Ecological Imperialism: The Biological Expansion of Europe, 900–1900*. *Biological* expansion of Europe? Imperialism as an *ecological* event? Yes, and therein lie the quiet clues to the connections we seek—*and* to the contestation around "sustainability" and "sustainable development" that goes on in the present. In due course we will have to slip even further back, to

Neolithic culture, in order to understand what happened to nature and culture in their common trek *to* the present and why they now live under a common threat *in* the present. But for now we begin exactly where Crosby does, on page 1. The book opens thus:

> European emigrants and their descendants are all over the place, which requires explanation.
> It is more difficult to account for the distribution of this subdivision of the human species than that of any other. The locations of the others make an obvious kind of sense. All but a relatively few of the members of the many varieties of Asians live in Asia. Black Africans live on three continents, but most of them are concentrated in their original latitudes, the tropics, facing each other across one ocean. Amerindians, with few exceptions, live in the Americas, and nearly every last Australian Aborigine dwells in Australia. Eskimos live in the circumpolar lands, and Melanesians, Polynesians, and Micronesians are scattered through the islands of only one ocean, albeit a large one. All these peoples have expanded geographically—have   committed acts of imperialism, if you will—but they have expanded into lands adjacent to or at least near to those in which they had already been living, or, in the case of the Pacific peoples, to the next island and then to the next after that, however many kilometers of water might lie between. Europeans, in contrast, seem to have leapfrogged around the globe.[6]

Or, in an image which Crosby takes from beekeeping, "Europeans . . . have swarmed again and again and have selected their new homes as if each swarm were physically repulsed by the others."[7]

Europeans have indeed swarmed, in two senses. Both are important to the biological expansion of Europe and ecological imperialism.

Europeans first swarmed as population. The highest population growth rates in recorded history are not those of Asians, Latin Americans or Africans, but Europeans in the period 1750–1930, that is, roughly the three centuries Stevens noted and which Smith, Marx and Engels, and Darwin at different times and in different ways documented. The number of Caucasians in this period increased over 5 times, as compared with a 2.3 increase for Asians and less than 2 for Africans (and African-Americans). In what Crosby calls the "Neo-Europes" (the places Europeans settled in leapfrogging around the world), the population between 1750–1930 increased phenomenally—more than 14 times over! The jump for the rest of the world was by comparison a paltry fraction—2.5 times. In the more recent slice of this period, from 1840–1930, the European population at home grew from 194 million to 463 million, still double the rate of increase of the rest of the world.[8]

During this same century the second "swarming" of Europeans occurred. Not population growth this time, but emigration. 1820–1930 saw "the deluge" (Crosby). Over fifty million Europeans migrated to establish or solidify "Neo-Europes" abroad. Recorded emigration has never happened on that scale, before or since. Fifty million people was in fact one fifth of the entire European population at the beginning of this period.[9]

What is happening here, and what counts as the significance of these swarmings? Certainly the conquest of "new worlds" is happening, and the establishment of Western sources for what today is misleadingly termed "globalization." Moreover, this state-of-affairs seems utterly taken-for-granted by Caucasians even as it turns transnational and multicultural. Crosby offers the aside that the thirty-million square kilometers of land secured by whites around the globe is one of the "very greatest aberrations in the demographic history of the species."[10] Aberrant or not, it is evidently "a situation this minority considers permanent."[11] Considered permanent as well, to recall Bruce Rich, is the "self-evident" organizing principle for every society and nation this side of the dual swarming—"economic development."

Yet to read the five hundred years since Columbus in the manner of raw political and economic imperialism *only*, as led by demographics, prevents us from seeing what we most need to see—history and nature, culture and environment impacted together and interlaced in ways both noticed and unnoticed. This certainly is the biological expansion of Europe in Neo-Europes around the world. But what is the history of nature as intertwined with peoples in this still unfinished saga?

Understand, first, two things: how strange the New World was to these alien swarms, and how confident they were about their mission of transformation, a transformation including nature.

As those who live on this side of the great nature-culture upending, we can only partially sense the strangeness of the new worlds for European emigrants. Some perspective is gained by standing on the Manhattan side of the Hudson River, anywhere from Riverside Park north to Inwood Park, and gazing across the waters to the New Jersey palisades. These cliffs, falling straightaway to the river, are a geological breach of millennial proportion (to understate it badly). This ancient rock exposed itself to the rest of creation at the coming apart of Pangaea, that enormous land mass from which all present continents are the leftovers. Continents huddled as Pangaea before slowly riding tectonic plates hither and yon, held afloat by plastic rock and, deep down, the molten fire beneath. So "East" New England is now West Europe, as "East" Brazil and the Caribbean are West and Central Africa.

Fascinating to latecomers like us as this may be, why is it important? Because nature evolved differently after the breakup of Pangaea's marriage and the Big Drift. The flora and fauna of one portion of the planet, and their diseases as well, were not a photocopy of other portions at all, even at the same latitude and clime. Nero, after all, threw Christians to the lions, not the cougars.[12] (Both Nero and his particular lions are now extinct, of course, but that is another matter.) Or, in another amusing example, a Mr. Martin from Great Britain complains as he visits Australia in the 1830s that the trees retained their leaves and shed their bark instead, the swans were black, the eagles white, the bees were stingless, some mammals had pockets, others laid eggs, it was warmest on the hills and coolest in the valleys, [and] even the blackberries were red.[13]

Noted from another angle, the very regions that today produce the majority of the foodstuffs of European provenance, grains and meats, had "no wheat, barley, rye, cattle, pigs, sheep, or goats whatsoever" five hundred years ago.[14] More than that, these particular grain-and meat-based systems have marginalized or exterminated almost all other forms of agricultural production worldwide, even though they themselves borrowed plenty from the New World and kept it as their own as we shall see.[15] Since about 1450, most of the agricultural systems of what we now call the third world have in fact experienced gradual genetic collapse.[16] We may think it quite "natural" that (immigrant) Argentineans, Brazilians, Costa Ricans, Hawaiians, Canadians, and Texans raise cattle to export to Europe, the United States, and Japan. But it is only "natural" in a European sense, just as to this day it has "naturally" never occurred to any European theologian or philosopher to contemplate what third world genetic collapse means for creation and its peoples. Only now, as transnational pharmaceutical, petro-agricultural and biotechnology firms are scrambling to locate and patent the remaining biogenetic material for the purposes of research, commerce, and profit, is this impacted and vastly altered nature suddenly an "issue" meriting international treaties and guaranteed access for "global" firms anchored in the Neo-Europes of the world.[17]

The point cannot be labored, only stated. Europeans are not a different species and are genetically no more or less expansionist than other peoples infected with material desire, the glories of heroism, the adventure of conquest, and the pleasure of killing unwanted neighbors. But Europeans were the first to learn to master the great ocean currents and winds and were thus the first to cross the seams of Pangaea en masse and in such a way as to stitch them shut. And they stitched them shut not only by acts of sociocultural imperialism, but ecological imperialism. Thus Crosby:

> The seams of Pangaea were closing, drawn together by the sailmaker's needle. Chickens met kiwis, cattle met kangaroos, Irish met potatoes, Comanches met horses, Incas met smallpox—all for the first time. The countdown to the extinction of the passenger pigeon and the native peoples of the Greater Antilles and of Tasmania had begun. A vast expansion in the numbers of certain other species on this planet began, led off by pigs and cattle, by certain weeds and pathogens, and by the Old World peoples who first benefited from contact with lands on the other side of the seams of Pangaea.[18]

"Drawn together by the sailmaker's needle" indeed! In 1492, the sailors first crossed the Atlantic in a way that "stuck" and a few years earlier, in 1488, that other marker of Smith, Darwin, Marx and Engels, the Cape of Good Hope, was rounded as ship after ship headed in the opposite direction. Only three decades later, the entire globe was circumnavigated and by 1600 private citizens, not just sailors, were on board for the journey.[19] It would only be a matter of time until Broadway would symbolize Progress as a cradled ship in the foyer of the New Amsterdam Theater. New Amsterdam, New York, the fate of the Manhattan Indians, and the Palisades testify to Pangaea's breakup. It is one very long history telescoped and climaxed by some few thousands of sailors over a few hundred years.

Yet understanding this as a transformation *of nature and culture together*, of the history of nature itself on a global scale, requires another kind of voyage; a voyage into the consciousness of these adventurers, into their habits of heart, into their convictions, religion, and way of life. And not just into the heads and hearts of adventurers at the helm or in the trading company offices of Marx's rising revolutionary bourgeoisie, but of private citizens as well, both the citizens who joined the mass emigrations and those who stayed home. After all, people do not live in raw nature so much as in their pictures of nature, nature as humanly "cognized." And people do not live in "cognized" nature only. To use an equally dreadful term, they live in nature as "operationalized," nature as it lives and dies in peoples' transformations of it. "Culture," Donna Haraway says, "designates the political realization of natural materials."[20] And so it is.

Samuel Purchas was one of those who unwittingly bore testimony to the intimacies of culture and nature in the human consciousness. A seventeenth-century Englishman of the cloth, this is his ode:

> who ever tooke possession of the huge Ocean, and made procession about the vast Earth? Who ever discovered new Constellations, saluted the Frozen Poles, subjected the Burning Zones? And who else by the Art of Navigation have seemed to imitate Him, which laies the beames of his chambers in the Waters, and walketh on the wings of the Wind?[21]

The answer, of course, is sailors, English sailors in the first instance. The alert exegete uncovers something else here, however, something so "natural" to Purchas that the images of praise almost offer themselves of their own accord. In their possession, procession and subjection, these sailors imitate none less than God. But which God, whose God? The God of the Book of Job and of the great creation Psalm, Psalm 104! "Him, which laies the beames of his chambers in the Waters, and walketh on the wings of the Wind." No chapters of the Bible and few in any literature anywhere so majestically describe the Creator of the Cosmos as these do. But they do so in a way carefully designed by the author of Job and the Psalmist to set the greatest possible distance between the majesty of the Creator and the creation, on the one hand, and the puniness, transiency, and vulnerability of humanity on the other. Precisely this God, the God of unsurpassing transcendence, of possession, procession, and subjection in *cos-*

mic degree, is the God whose work, to Purchas's mind, compares favorably with little English sailors in small boats on high seas on dangerous voyages! Were we not all now and again familiar with such "innocent" arrogance and an ability to turn argument and fact on their heads, it would be hard to imagine how such comparisons and conceits could be conceived and held.

Consider other texts. One is the fourth citation from Crosby's frontispiece. It, too, belongs to a famous scholar, Charles Lyell, from his *Principles of Geology* of 1832: "Yet, if we wield the sword of extermination as we advance, we have no reason to repine the havoc committed."[22] Crosby might also have used a line from a great nature conservationist, hunter and U.S. president, Theodore Roosevelt. "The settler and the pioneer," he wrote in *The Winning of the West*, "have at bottom had justice on their side. This great continent could not have been kept as nothing but a game preserve for squalid savages."[23]

The last text is lengthier and in two parts. The first is from Kiowa nation history, the second from the English governor in the Neo-Europe of Massachusetts. Both are about smallpox in a part of Pangaea that had never known it.

The Kiowa are a people of the Great Plains of North America. In one account the mythic hero of the nation, Saynday, comes across a stranger. The stranger is dressed in a black suit and wears a tall hat, the dress of Christian missionaries known to the Kiowa. The stranger speaks first.

"Who are you?"
"I'm Saynday. I'm the Kiowa's Old Uncle Saynday. I'm the one who's always coming along. Who are you?"
"I'm smallpox."
"Where do you come from and what do you do and why are you here?"
"I come from far away, across the Eastern Ocean. I am one with the white men—they are my people as the Kiowas are yours. Sometimes I travel ahead of them, and sometimes I lurk behind. But I am always their compan-

ion and you will find me in their camps and in their houses."

"What do you do?"

"I bring death. My breath causes children to wither like young plants in the spring snow. I bring destruction. No matter how beautiful a woman is, once she has looked at me she becomes as ugly as death. And to men I bring not death alone but the destruction of their children and the blighting of their wives. The strongest warriors go down before me. No people who have looked at me will ever be the same."[24]

Thus the old story of the Kiowa, told in the language of dreamy myth but raw with the experience of history. Crosby, in next citing John Winthrop, fabled first governor of Massachusetts Bay Colony, comments that "the whites took a sunnier view of imported diseases." He then quotes lawyer Winthrop from May, 1634: "For the natives, they are neere all dead of small Poxe, so as the Lord hathe cleared our title to what we possess."[25]

Taking title by such means, with such sanction, occupies the same universe and way of life as the possession and procession of European sailors in their faithful imitation of the great God Jehovah. The same consciousness of all things transformed, land and peoples alike and together, runs in the cultural bloodstream of these peoples as they press the sacred cause of "civilization," a cause laid on them by "the Laws of Nature and Nature's God."[26] The same consciousness was also part of a later episode with native peoples and smallpox, when U.S. Cavalry traded blankets they first infected with smallpox.

To most of those long at home in this place, this did not look like "civilization." To all but the Europeans, it was "predatory expansive agriculture and parasitic resource use"[27] cast in the mythology of expanding frontiers and manifest destiny. And it put in place the grand illusion that the West has lived from since and now globalizes. In Timothy Weiskel's words, "Having expanded upon the things in nature, the West came to believe that expansion was in the nature of things. Perpetual growth was considered natural, good, and inevitable."[28] To this day, Weiskel adds, "we are trying to sustain a 'frontier culture' in a post-frontier world."[29] The expansionist vision lives on even though earth is no longer flat. Differently said, a life without limits in a world of our own making (globalized European) was the dream and drive of modernity from its very beginning, long before Ronald Reagan and the invention of the first neoconservative. Even in its most calamitous moments, after the Great War and during the Great Depression, the World's Fair in Chicago could still confidently proclaim "A Century of Progress." Promethean power for the transformation of nature and culture together via economic messianism is modernity's very soul and pulse. The difference between 1492, 1776, and the present is that the transformation is now fully institutionalized, globalized, and "self-evident[ly]" organized as "economic development" (Rich). It will not be easily dissuaded, much less rooted out. The bulk of Adam Smith's library, after all, is not in his native Scotland, or England, or even the University of Texas. It is in Tokyo.

For his part Crosby uses the delightful image of Sweet Betsy to draw the tale together. In one sense, it is inappropriate, since the long trek of neo-European globalization has been overwhelmingly male-minded and male-led. At the same time, Sweet Betsy and her entourage capture in one image the biological expansion and ecological imperialism of Europe together with its cultural expansion and imperialism. Crosby's source is, of course, the favorite frontier folksong, "Sweet Betsy from Pike." Betsy herself was from Pike County, Missouri, and she crossed the high mountains, the Rockies, with her lover Ike. Not only Ike, however, but "two yoke of oxen, a large yellow dog, a tall shanghai rooster, and one spotted hog." As Crosby notes:

> Betsy was heir to a very old tradition of mixed farming, and whereas it must be pointed out that her oxen were castrated and the other animals without mates, Betsy's

party was not the only one to cross the mountains; wagon trains had bulls and cows, plus hens and dogs and pigs of genders opposite to those of her animals. (Betsy herself had the foresight to bring Ike.) Rapid propagation of the colonizing species would be the rule on the far side of the mountains. Betsy came not as an individual immigrant but as part of a grunting, lowing, neighing, crowing, chirping, snarling, buzzing, self-replicating and world-altering avalanche.[30]

This, then, is the outcome of the past five centuries: a "world-altering avalanche" that slid outward from Europe and has upended culture and nature together. Such is the proper context for discussing sustainability, population, and development.

Yet even this bead on what brought us from "there" to "here" is gauged too narrowly. Present predicaments, and the issues of sustainability and the play of human power, require a deeper, broader gaze.

FOUR REVOLUTIONS OR THREE?

The Annual Review of the Canadian Round Table hopes that we are now entering the world's fourth great revolution. (The Canadians, irrepressible *homo sapiens* that they are, mean the *human* world's fourth revolution.) The first three were the agricultural, the industrial, and the informational. These cover human history from approximately 10,000–8000 B.C.E. to the present and into the foreseeable future, a story arching from life in neolithic villages to present megacities. These revolutions all shared one crucial characteristic that determined the basic contours of our present world. They all *reorganized society* so as *to produce more effectively*.[31] To do so, and quite unlike most hunter-gatherers, the peoples of these revolutions self-consciously *reconfigured nature for the sake of society*. Society was a set-apart, humanly designed, humanly ordered rendition of nature.

The fourth great revolution is the one which has not yet

come to pass, but must, for survival's sake. ("If current trends continue, we will not," to borrow Daniel Maguire's crisp formula.)[32] It is the ecological revolution and its social-economic characteristic is qualitatively different. Namely, to "reorganize society to produce without destructiveness."[33] We must add "and *reproduce* without destructiveness," since a rising human population, especially at high levels of consumption, is a sure and heavy multiplier of all socioenvironmental problems.

Yet neither the Canadians nor the rest of us have much idea about the shape of mandatory, nonviolent systems that yield sustainable societies, that is, society without destructiveness. We have little notion of what such an imperative means for our daily habits and consciousness, our worldviews and ethics, or for organizing a world that can sustain six, then eight, perhaps ten billion people, all in the normal lifetime of a child born in the Northern Hemisphere in the 1990s.[34] We are stymied before the question of what this social revolution implies for current and alternative moral, philosophical, and religious visions, and for our institutions, polities, policies, and laws. With all the goodwill on earth, we nonetheless balk at the pastoral issues before us: What kind of life together buoys hope, clears the eyes, and draws us out of our tribalisms when greater constraint on all sides is the common experience? What structures of daily life and devotion let grace and the mystery of life wash our grimy souls, nudge courage, enable sacrifice, arouse the heart, and fire the imagination, just when millions grieve over diminished dreams and clutch at what little (or much) they have? How, in the end, do we learn, decide, and act prudently in the face of sure uncertainty and risk, within more crowded parameters? Primarily religious and ethical questions, they are somewhere near center for the transition to the Canadians' hoped-for fourth revolution.

Yet whatever our responses, they must include understanding the three revolutions that have brought us thus far on the way. We take each in turn.

NEOLITHIC REVOLUTIONARIES

The shift to agricultural societies seems to have happened in three separate areas simultaneously: southwest Asia, China, and Mesoamerica. On some counts, this must be reckoned the most important transition in human history. Called the Neolithic Revolution, it was actually several revolutions dotting four or five thousand years. The growth of settled societies, the emergence of cities and of craft specializations, the rise of powerful religions and philosophies with accompanying social elites, the development of writing, horticulture, pottery, weaving, and many of the arts, the domestication of animals and plants—all this belongs to the Neolithic Revolution. (By about 2000 B.C.E. all the major crops and animals that belong to present agricultural systems around the world had been domesticated, even though the agricultural systems themselves were drastically changed and relocated after the neolithic revolutions.)[35]

Not the least of neolithic innovations was population growth. After about 5000 B.C.E., the upward trend in human population, modest though it was, began and has continued ever since. This all happened in societies which established culture as agriculture and village life as the normal context for human development, even though some impressive urban centers also emerged.[36] (The legacy of village life, too, extended well into the modern era. It is the lot of hundreds of millions still.)

Yet lines drawn too sharply between hunter-gatherer and agricultural society falsify the record. Hunter-gatherers were not passive toward their environment. They also intervened in ways affecting the ecosystems of their locales. They followed animal populations and practiced controlled predation, sometimes virtually "herding" these wild populations, just as they sometimes seeded plants in the "wild" (our notion, not theirs) and engaged in limited small-scale irrigation. It now appears that not only dogs but pigs were domesticated before crops and settled agriculture.[37] Apparently basketry and some weaving predate the Neolithic Revolution as well.[38]

All this said, the agricultural transition was nonetheless a transformation that radically changed society and nature together. Ponting's summary extends ours.

> The development of agriculture, bringing with it inten-sive forms of food production and settled societies, had essentially the same effect all over the world. Surplus food was used to feed a growing religious and political elite and a class of craftsmen whose main role was to sup-ply that elite. The redistribution of surplus food required extensive control mechanisms for transport, storage and reissue leading to powerful central institutions within society. These processes became self-reinforcing as the elites with political and social power took an ever greater degree of control and imposed greater discipline through enforced labour and service, first in labour gangs for major social projects such as temples or irrigation works and then in the rapidly growing armies. Societies that were broadly egalitarian were replaced by ones with dis-tinct classes and huge differences in wealth.[39]

Ponting goes on to note two further consequences, one positive, one negative. Both have formed history into the pre-sent. Virtually all major human cultural and intellectual achievements would have been impossible without the development of agriculture and a food surplus. The develop-ment of whole worlds of art, science, and culture followed from the fact that a growing number of people were no longer engaged in the direct production of food. Builders, architects, artists, priests, philosophers, and scientists, together with their creations, were invented.[40]

A parallel development was increased coercion within society and warfare between societies. The great projects of these societies were only possible with huge amounts of human labor. Lacking sufficient volunteers, some wielded power and authority over others.

Also, settled societies meant defined territories and the ownership and control of resources. This increased the reasons and potential for jostling with the neighbors, and out-and-out warfare. (By about 7500 B.C.E., Jericho had a wall almost half a mile long around it, 10 feet thick and 13 feet high, with at least one tower 30 feet in diameter and 28 feet high.[41] Megiddo, on the Plain of Armageddon, had been destroyed and rebuilt twenty times before B.C.E. saw the dawn of C.E.)[42]

Ponting's conclusion overall, directed to our issues of sustainability and the play of human power, is that societies this side of the agricultural revolution provide the first examples of two phenomena we meet regularly *from neolithic times forward*: intensive human alteration of the environment, sometimes with major destructive impact; and the first societies which so damage the environment that they bring social collapse on themselves.[43]

All we need reiterate further is Crosby's point that the neolithic revolutions happened after the long, hard breakup of Pangaea (it took millions of years). Thus the evolution of plants and animals, both with and without human intervention, took place with different results in different locales, the greatest differences often across the greatest expanses of water. This includes evolved diseases and immunities, as well as new crops, "weeds" and "vermin" (both inventions of agriculture and settled communities), and animal species. When the seams of Pangaea are then stitched shut by sailors' needles, and their cargo of culture, crops, animals, and home-grown pathogens is off loaded, the new explorers, extractors, and settlers will not only have different ways, means, and intentions for ordering the world they find, they will also carry "the advantage of their infections."[44] (Before Crosby, William McNeill argued that the conquering of one people over another has had less to do with the technical and scientific advantages of "more advanced" or "developed" peoples over "less advanced" or "less developed" ones than the pestilence brought by one population to the vulnerabilities of another. Pestilence most often took the form of diseases. But it could, as Crosby documents over and again, take the form of feral plants and animals as well.)[45]

Yet pestilence is not the story. The story is the dynamic unsettling and resettling of nature and culture together since the agricultural revolution and by means of it. The story is sustainability and unsustainability. And in an era of mass, mechanized, petroleum-based agriculture, that is, agriculture as an industry, not the least important question is this: What kind of agriculture can sustain a world of six billion and more who belong to a species at the very top of the food chain? The answer is important for all, since none of us can live in a postagricultural world.

INDUSTRY

The industrial revolution is the second enumerated by the Canadians. Its success and power are manifest. In the words of the Catholic theologian of capitalism, Michael Novak: "No system has so revolutionized ordinary expectations of human life—lengthened the life span, made the elimination of poverty and famine thinkable, enlarged the range of human choice—as democratic capitalism."[46] Of course, the industrial revolution is more than democratic capitalism, or any other kind. But Novak's unchecked applause for capitalism holds for industrialization generally. The revolutionized expectations he praises have come in a way that generates unsustainability, however. (A subject that, we add, is missing in Novak's impressive output. Like the people, systems and economic culture he praises, Novak's thought, joining that of most neoconservatives, is ecologically empty.)

As has been amply demonstrated, industrial ecology lives by economic principles and practices that run against the grain of nature's own economy and literally undermine it. Industrial economies rarely even ask what nature requires for its own regeneration and renewal, much less align with those requirements. In addition, industrial ecology, with its tendencies to urbanize human settlements and appropriate carrying capacity from elsewhere through commerce, puts the consequences of its drastic reconfigurations of nature out of the sight of most people and thus out of mind as well. With that, urban peoples' sense of responsibility for the nature they depend on is quietly put to sleep.

What other dynamics prevail? The agricultural revolution prepared the way for the industrial in that it created settled human communities in which not all persons needed to be engaged in securing food and shelter. Bringing more land under cultivation and intensifying the means of cultivation also went hand-in-hand with a dramatic increase in human population. (The estimate is that after two million years of hunter-gatherer societies the population at the onset of agriculture ten thousand years ago was only four million.)[47] The industrial revolution quickened these trends dramatically. With the use of other energy sources, chiefly fossil fuels, and the spread of industrial production, far more persons could be, and were, engaged in nonagricultural endeavors at the same time that the basic needs of far more persons could be, and were, met (not least through the industrialization of agriculture itself). The resulting "population explosion" is strictly a phenomenon of the past two hundred years. Improvements in health and life span, higher agricultural production, a growing, now massive, place for creative commerce, industry and services, and the production and distribution of unprecedented wealth through them brought a soaring birthrate and longer lives. The drop in infant mortality rates and explosive growth of population in fact correlates with only one major development in human history: industrialization.[48] (From 1800 to the present, human population increased fivefold. In the 1980s earth had to support about ninety million more people *each year;* ninety million was the approximate *total* population of earth twenty-five hundred years ago.)[49]

Described somewhat differently, commerce and culture in agricultural societies and before the industrial revolution were regulated almost entirely by natural energy flows, chiefly solar energy as captured by food, wood, and wind. The industrial revolution, by contrast, came about through the use of *stored* energy (fossil fuels).[50] As Hawken notes, this permitted a hardly noticed, but huge transition. Commerce and culture could shift from necessarily working *with* natural forces to *overcoming them* for human ends. Production processes and people could both be separated from intrinsic ties to land. An artificial or artifactual world could be created, with few constraints from the very nature on which it depended utterly. It buried that nature *in* the artifacts themselves or in the processes of their production, distribution, and consumption. The economy of nature will no doubt have the last word in all this. But for the time being industrial ecology had found the way, through stored energy and processes of industrialization, commerce, and trade, to massively reconfigure nature for the sake of *and as* human society.

INDUSTRIAL CULTURE

Because industrialism reconfigured nature as society in a certain way, it became a culture as well. For human beings, culture is "second nature." And industrial culture is now so much a part of the skin we live in that we hardly notice its uniqueness in earth's story. We do not have community and society, Wendell Berry says in a slightly different context, so much as "industry": "the power industry, the defense industry, the communications industry, the transportation industry, the agriculture industry, the food industry, the health industry, the entertainment industry, the mining industry, the education industry, the law industry, the government industry, and the religion industry."[51]

So accustomed are we to this massively reconfigured world of nature and culture together that we barely recognize its difference from all that went before. In the economy of nature and in most of human history (hunter-gatherer society) all creatures consume *only* renewable resources—fruit, nuts, plants, fish and animals, seeds, grass, berries, bark, and so on. Industrial society, however, draws from stored energy to use both renewable *and* nonrenewable resources (and renewables at a nonrenewable rate). The capacity to do so is called progress. And for multitudes (of humans), it has been just that. But as Hawken notes, we should realize what progress fueled in this way now means. "Every day the world-wide economy burns an amount of energy the planet required ten thousand days to create. Or, put another way, twenty-seven years worth of stored solar energy is burned and released by utilities, cars, houses, factories, and farms every twenty-four hours."[52] It hardly takes rocket scientist intelligence to read "unsustainability" writ large here, if such a way of life goes on for very long, in earth terms, or if very large numbers of persons pursue it even a short while. "No deposit, no return" as a way of life cannot work.

Still, from a human point of view abstracted from the rest of nature, industrialization looked like genuine progress and was named as such. After all, with "industriousness" humans could modify and control their environments in ways that met the needs of more and more people. It offered many far greater choices, longer lives, more adventure, new freedoms and opportunities. Whole new worlds were created and inhabited, with increased well-being for millions.

From an ecological point of view, however, what was happening was very different. To earth, industrialization looks more and more like a succession of more complex and environmentally disruptive and damaging ways to meet the needs and wants of one inordinately aggressive species. From the ground up, that is, from earth, industrialization is speedier deforestation; soil erosion and salinization; desertification; loss of life, even entire species; decrease of the genetic pool; higher levels of and new kinds of pollution and other waste; the destruction of cultures and even peoples alien to modernity; and highly unequal distribution of wealth and resources, including food itself.[53]

So it can hardly come as a surprise that the chief relationship of "industrious" humans to the rest of nature is domination and alienation. Industrialization's mighty victories and extensive benefits have, in fact, been won precisely *through alienation*: humans are the subjects and the rest of nature is comprised of fundamentally "other" objects. *And through domination*: humans overcome natural constraints in order to exploit nature for human ends. (This is the message of those prototypical modern philosophers, Francis Bacon and Réné Descartes, i.e., knowledge is mastery and "objective" representation is the most reliable form of truth.) These in turn are the keys to human power and control over (the rest of) nature.[54]

It should not come as a surprise that this revolution overturns deeply ingrained ways of societies whose living is "closer to the land." Culture is *never* severed from nature or nature from culture, so cultures whose ways of life were intimate with nature on *pre*industrial terms were as much the object of domination by industrialism as the rest of nature. (Darwin's "wherever the European has trod, death seems to pursue the aboriginal.") So, too, matters of gender, in which women were perceived as "closer to nature" and thus in need of subjection to men, who were more possessed of "mind" and "reason." In short, the conflict of cultures necessarily included conflict with different notions of nature and different uses of it.

But what kind of culture is industrialism? It is first of all a dream and a promise—to supplant poverty, disease, and toil with an abundance that permits the good life as enriching, expanded choice. That dream and promise (and partial success) has been irresistible and remains the lure. Industrialism is also a way of life, one of economic materialism and market rationality (Berry's "industry") with a certain set of cultural assumptions. We simply list the assumptions underpinning this way of life.

- Nature has a virtually limitless storehouse of resources for human use.
- Humanity has the commission to use and control nature.
- Nature is malleable and can be reconfigured for human ends.
- Humanity has the right to use nature's resources for an ongoing improvement in the material standard of living.
- The most effective way to assume the continuing elevation of material standards of living is through ongoing economic growth.

- The quality of life itself is furthered by an economic system directed to ever-expanding material abundance.
- The future is open, systematic material progress for the whole human race is possible, and through the careful use of human powers humanity can make history turn out right.
- Human failures can be overcome through effective problem-solving.
- Problem-solving will be effective if reason and goodwill are present, and science and technology are developed and applied in a free environment.
- Science and technology are neutral means for serving human ends.
- Modern science and technology have helped achieve a superior civilization in the West.
- What can be scientifically known and technologically done should be known and done.
- The things we create are under our control.
- The good life is one of productive labor and material well-being.
- The successful person is the one who achieves.
- Both social progress and individual interests are best served by achievement-oriented behavior in a competitive and entrepreneurial environment.
- A work ethic is essential to human satisfaction and social progress.
- The diligent, hardworking, risk-taking, and educated will attain their goals.
- There is freedom in material abundance.
- When people have more, their freedom of choice is expanded and they can and will *be* more.[55]

All this is a distant cousin of the amusing entry in a seventeenth-century European diary: "I'd rather face a thousand attacking Turks than one Calvinist bent on doing the will of God." Not that this culture is parochially Calvinist! It is more decidedly ecumenical. Frederic Morton's *Crosstown Sabbath*, narrating the experience of riding the Forty-second Street crosstown bus in New York, describes the fatigue on

the faces of the passengers as "classically Judeo-Christian."
We are imitating the God of our civilization, Morton says,
the "Workaholic Supernal" who "assembled the world in
Factory terms." "Before the Hebrews, no other people had a
sabbath," he writes. "No other people needed one."[56]

Yet this culture did not emerge from the pages of Genesis or even Calvin's Reformation, whatever contributions
were theirs. Nor did the industrial revolution, quite unlike
the agricultural, develop separately and independently in different parts of the globe simultaneously. It was a process and
culture dominated at the start by one part of the world,
Europe, then exported and extended through the network of
the Neo-Europes, and chiefly North America. Of late some
Asian countries have come to play a large role as well. Industrialization took a couple of hundred years to develop in
Europe and the Neo-Europes, a mere wink of an eye in earth
time. But it took less than a wink elsewhere because its base
was in place, experience had developed tested and trans-
portable processes, and the earlier episode of conquest and
colonization put in place a ready global infrastructure with
essential links from centers to margins. This now includes a
multiracial and multiethnic elite serving a wider, shared
Western industrialized culture.

Understanding this genealogy is vital. It means that both
nature and culture have come under increasing control of the
West over the past five centuries and especially the past two
(industrialization's best working years). Industrialized countries have thus established access to the resources of virtually
the whole world through economic processes they continue
to dominate, now quite apart from direct political control or
Western zip codes. (Once expected to be *the* big story of the
twentieth century, decolonization dwindles more and more
as the story of autonomy and independence.)

All this was a dramatic change from all previous human
arrangements, when, despite considerable and even distant
trade, societies were dependent for most all their significant
ends *on the resources of their own area* and the use of *renewable resources only.*

DEVELOPMENT AND CORPORATIONS

We must return to the "civilizational" change wrought by industrialism as led by the West, and overwhelmingly by men. The process by which preindustrial societies become industrial ones has come to be called "development." A synonym for economic progress, it was, until the ecocrisis, taken for granted as the proper course for societies wishing to enter the modern world. Such development is now so extensive and widely accepted that it is no longer considered parochial, but global. It is Rich's "self-evident" organizing principle of modern societies.[57] All the international gatherings of the United Nations in the 1990s have assumed its validity, needing only to add "sustainable" as an important front-end adjective.

Yet "globalization," "the global economy," and "development" are misleading terms. They mask the ways in which development and progress belong to a highly particular culture with specific assumptions and values (the list above) and a very short tenure in earth history. As we have seen, it is a culture that uses and dominates nature (and people it views as "close to nature") and alienates humanity from the rest of nature (and people from one another on the basis of a certain socialization). In addition, its critics claim it has learned certain attitudinal incapacities in the process of disenchanting the world. Chiefly, this is the incapacity to receive the world as gift and to stand in utter awe and celebration of life as holy mystery and gift. Apparently industrial culture's assumptions convinced us that we are life's creators and keepers. For a species not given to fine-tuned perfection, this is hubris (more male than female) of disastrous dimensions.

But what about the industrial revolution's institutions? The key new institution, it turns out, was not the one usually cited, the nation-state, despite the fact it arose near the beginning of the industrial revolution and became an active and critical player. (Nation-statehood as a modern form of sovereignty is usually dated to the Peace of Westphalia of

1648.) The key institution was not even much noted when it was born. It was the corporation as "the little engine that could." Like that engine, it led the rest of the economic train up the mountain, over it, and down the other side, with an avalanche in tow.

The corporation was a brilliant invention that unleashed a new spirit of enterprise in a particularly potent form. Its history is fascinating and important.

Corporations developed in the fifteenth and sixteenth centuries, about the time sailors were stitching shut the seams of Pangaea. Debts then were transgenerational. That meant children and other relatives bore liability for debts of the ancestors and could land in debtors' prisons for the "sins of the fathers unto the third and fourth generation." And they often did. But in order to sponsor exploration of the New World, England chartered corporations with a distinctive, powerful new provision: limited liability. If ships with their precious cargoes were lost to bad weather or piracy, or simply lost, stockholders' liabilities were limited to the investment they had made and no more. With such state-sponsored corporations, commerce found the form which did two vital things at once: absorbed risk-taking and promoted exploration and settlement (the Neo-Europes). The charter of limited liability, unique among forms of enterprise, was a dazzling innovation unwittingly tailor-made for the transition from agricultural societies to globalizing commerce and industrialism.[58]

Initially the corporation was subordinate to its sturdy sponsor, the state. This meant strict limits stipulated in the corporation charter itself: limits on profits, indebtedness and overall capitalization, together with the amount of land that could be acquired.[59] As late as the nineteenth century, corporations were considered, in the language of U.S. statutes, a "creature of the law and may be molded to any shape or for any purpose that the Legislature may deem most conducive for the general good."[60]

The U.S. Supreme Court's interpretation of the Fourteenth Amendment, meant to protect the rights of freed slaves, changed the status and power of corporations dramatically, however. Corporations now enjoyed the same status before the law as individual persons. On this basis hundreds, perhaps thousands, of state laws and regulations were overturned: on wages, working conditions, ownership, and capitalization. Since that ruling corporations have found even more latitude to take risks far beyond their original borders. Before long they came not simply to join nation-states jockeying for global economic benefit but to create the global competition for resources and profits themselves. In fact, a spectacular turnabout occurred, and nation-states now vie to be included in the wealth generated by corporations in the global economy. "When it comes to global markets these days," a *New York Times* article says, "the motto of governments is: 'There they go, I must catch up, for I am their leader.'"[61]

The issue at this point is not corporations per se, however. It is the huge role they have come to play in the Industrial Revolution's exploration and extraction of world resources, the settlement and flourishing of the Neo-Europes, the growth of trade, the globalization of production, the flow of technology and finance, and the promotion of living styles, ideologies, and values promotive of these processes. As of the 1990s the whole world has become a kind of "non-union hiring hall"[62] for these giants as they have become the effective working matrix for what they casually combine as "human" and "natural" "capital" and "resources." Their economic clout is enormous on its own terms: in the 1990s the one hundred largest corporations in the world had more economic power than 80 percent of the world's people![63] Perhaps exaggerated at the time, Maurer's description from the mid-1950s, with its solar system metaphor, no longer exaggerates at all.

> The large corporation might better be imagined as a gravitational body, around which revolve several planets in roughly established orbits. In the primary series of orbits are members of the corporate community itself:

directors, managers, executives of various degrees, and wage-earners. In the secondary group of orbits are consumers, the public in general, competitors, dealers, distributors, sub-contractors, suppliers and stockholders. In a third and somewhat erratic orbit lies the federal government, in company with the governments of foreign countries in which the corporation operates.[64]

The role of corporations is equally significant for the third revolution—the informational. But before turning to that, a concluding comment about industrialism is in order, together with two stories.

COMMENT

The oft-heard thesis is that we live in a "postindustrial" society and age. The relative decline in heavy industry and factory production (smoke as progress) and the surge of new ventures and jobs in services and high technology is given as the sure evidence. Some of this—the surge of new ventures— is part and parcel of the information revolution and is arguably "postindustrial." But the term and thesis are deceptive. It is certainly true that the industrial revolution itself means that more of the population can be supported in non-industrial occupations. New services and livelihoods can grow and older ones can be extended with the dividends of an expanding industrial economy.

It is also true that industrial employment is going the way of agricultural employment. In that sense, too, we may be "postindustrial." In the middle of the nineteenth century in the United States, for example, a *majority* of the population was engaged in agriculture. By 1900 that had dropped to a third, by 1940 to a fifth, and today just under 3 percent. The U.S. is not exceptional; by 1990 no developed country had more than 5 percent of the work force in farming. Moreover, with the exception of Japan, none of the developed countries was a heavy net importer of food. In fact, the work force is way down, farm production is up, and both of these were achieved through the industrialization of agriculture. Agribusiness is in fact one of the most capital-intensive, technology-intensive, and information-intensive industries around.[65]

Yet the point is that the same pattern is developing in other industrial sectors. Between 1960 and 1990, production of manufactured goods of all types continued to rise, but the jobs required for that flow dropped by half. U.S. industrial production grew faster than in any other developed country except Japan in the very same decades (1960–1990) that the industrial work force shrunk faster than in any other developed country.[66] Services, an exploding sector during this season, generated enough jobs to plug the largest part of the employment gap. (By 1990 perhaps as many as 90 million jobs in the United States alone were in services, enough to say that this sector saved us from devastating unemployment.[67]) Nonetheless, on a *global* scale, unemployment is at the highest levels since the great depression of the 1930s, somewhere in the neighborhood of eight hundred million unemployed and underemployed.[68] Peter Drucker concludes that one of the twentieth century's big stories is the rise and demise of the blue-collar worker. No class has risen faster, he says, and none has fallen so precipitously.[69]

In short, the exodus from agriculture and other industries has led to the thesis that we live in a "postindustrial age." The grand deception, however, is that "postindustrial" means less industrial production. It emphatically does not. In fact, industrialization is expanding greatly, as are the amounts of resources and energy consumed, significant efficiencies notwithstanding. The flow of natural capital into manufactured capital is not declining, it is increasing. And the call is for much more of the same, so that "developing countries" might become "developed" at high levels of goods and services. Sustainable development depends on this. The U.N.-sponsored Brundtland Commission report says five to ten times the current economic activity is needed! Yes, certain communities, even societies and nations, may experience not only new (informational) industries but *de*industrialization as well. Yet when they do, their response is not to welcome and assist it but to fight it. The struggle for industry, including heavy industry, normally *intensifies*. Economic growth must be put "back on track," retain precious jobs, and make up for lost ones. Industrialization, like agriculture, has changed significantly. But through the changes, it, again like agriculture, has always sought to expand and intensify, and has largely succeeded. (Incidentally, of the 5.4 million people employed abroad by U.S. corporations alone, 80 percent are in manufacturing.[70]) This success, which is much closer to "hyper"-industrialization than "post-," is the chief reason *both* for unprecedented wealth *and* earth's distress. Ironically, and cruelly, this second human revolution has contributed the most *both* to human well-being and to unsustainability. Which is not only to say that here is another case of human advance and ruin residing in the same exercise of collective genius; it is to realize that this most generous of all revolutions cannot continue in the form we have come to know and depend on. It speaks only a few syllables in the last sentence of the most recent volume of earth history to date but they have been the most powerful and unsettling utterances of all. For population policy to depend on greatly increased production and consumption on this model is a solution which is not a solution. "Unsustainability" is stamped all over it.

STORIES

The first of the two stories will not make immediate sense to industrial culture people. That is its point. It reveals the coming revolution from the perspective of a *pre*industrial culture. (The story was recorded more than four hundred years ago.) The words are of an elderly Tupinamba "Indian" as recorded by the Frenchman, Jean de Lery. The French at the time (the 1500s) were battling the Portuguese and Dutch for control of the seas and the conquest of what was then called Pau-Brasil, now Brazil. (Pau-Brasil was the signature tree of Brazil. It is now largely extinct in areas the Europeans developed.) Jean de Lery recorded the following.

An old Indian once asked me: "Why do you come so far in search of wood to heat yourselves? Don't you have wood on your land?"

I told him we had a lot, but not of the same quality, and that we did not burn it but extracted color tints. I added that in our country there were traders who possessed more cloth, knives, scissors, mirrors, and other merchandise than he could even imagine, and that one of these traders bought the whole of Pau-Brasil with the laden cargoes of many ships.

"Ah," said the savage, "you're telling me tales of marvels . . . but this rich man you're talking about, won't he die?"

Yes, he'll die just like everyone else.

"And when he dies, to whom will he leave all he owns?"

To his sons, if he has any.

"Well," continued the Tupinamba, "I see now that you're all mad. You cross the seas, suffer all sorts of upsets, and work so hard to amass riches which you leave to your sons and those who live on. Don't tell me that the land you feed couldn't also feed you? We have our fathers, mothers, and sons that we love, but we believe that when we die the earth that has nurtured us will also nurture them. That's why we rest easy."[71]

The second story continues the first. It is also "Pau-Brazil," a century and two and three later. This is Brazil as depicted in the huge murals of the Palacio Tiradentes, the ornate, lavish parliament building in Rio de Janeiro which was once the national parliament building but is now home to the provincial parliament. The occasion for this writer's presence was the Earth Summit and the report of Stephen Schmidheiny of the Business Council for Sustainable Development to the Global Forum of Spiritual and Parliamentary Leaders on Human Survival. Before Schmidheiny's report, we all participated in a joint North American meditation led by a Swami (from Boston), an Imam (from Baltimore), a Native

American chief (from upstate New York), and a Roman
Catholic sister (from Manhattan). Together they shared an
Omaha Indian prayer. Then Schmidheiny spoke of the global
business community's responsibility for environmentally
sustainable development. As he did I pondered the murals at
the base of the cupola and the oversize portrait of the first
assembly of Brazil. The first assembly was white, vested,
well-mustachioed, and neo-European to a man and the
murals were the more or less official history of Brazil, certainly the one that counted. Together the murals pictured the
procession of settlement and civilization come to the New
World. The Europeans were in white, arriving in long wagon
trains. They were led by a priest processing with a crucifix.
As they entered "Indian" villages evangelizing, they were
eagerly welcomed.

But what was striking to the wandering eye was high
above Schmidheiny and oblivious to his words. Just over the
ornate arch and probably ten feet tall was a stark, agonized
Christ, gray, skinny, dusty, suspended on a cross. It was a
striking commentary on power as Jesus hung dead-center
above the portrait of the first assembly and the Neo-European
procession. But most astounding of all for a tortured figure
hanging amid palatial splendor, the crucifix was considered
the natural expression of the culture and faith of those who
brought civilization and salvation to the indigenous peoples
of the "New World." So at home was this incongruency that
it was not seen as incongruous at all.

Schmidheiny's report on business-led sustainable development was followed by a panel representing corporations,
science, the arts, news media, women and youth, and a nice
earth song by John Denver.

INFORMATION AND RESOURCES

The basic assumptions of the Information Revolution do
not wander far those of the Industrial Revolution, at least not
at first glance: knowledge is power, power is control, and
growth is only limited by human imagination and access to

knowledge. It is particular knowledge, however—information about how things are "coded," work, and can evolve. What Frank Parsons was serious about in 1894 (see below) belongs to the hubris of the information age as much as the "sensible industrial system" he intended. The Information Revolution in fact extends industrial hubris in assuming that all things, including biological mechanisms, are raw material for social manipulation. There is nothing, biological life included, which human beings cannot first decode and then "program" or "reprogram" for human ends.

Yet there are new twists that justify the word "revolution." Parsons in 1894:

> Life can be moulded into any conceivable form. Draw up your specifications for a dog, or a man . . . and if you will give me control of the environment, and time enough, I will clothe your dreams in flesh and blood . . . A sensible industrial system will seek to put men, as well as timber, stone, and iron, in the places for which their natures fit them, and to polish them for efficient service with at least as much care as is bestowed upon clocks, electric dynamos, or locomotives.[72]

"Timber, stone, and iron," together with "men," are not all that can be "polish[ed] . . . for efficient service" now. The Information Revolution lets us combine the organic and the technological in potentially endless configurations. With knowledge of life "codes," not least DNA and RNA, we might reinvent nature itself to solve the problems brought on us through inadequate information, harmful practices, and nature's nasty irregularities.

The cutting-edge technologies here are communications technologies and biotechnologies. Through bioengineering, nanotechnology, robotics, and computerization we might, for example, create molecules that feed on pollution and produce ozone, engineer foods with genes that delay decay or banish cholesterol, alter plants to fix their own fertilizer, banish bad genes that afflict us or other creatures with every successful reproduction, and patch ailing organisms and whole ecosystems with the right doses of creations tailored just for them. The organic is not opposed to the technological and artifactual here. It is the partner for the "one flesh" of a truly good marriage. Nature is the open-ended, unlimited resource for culture, and information culture is the resource for a new nature.

Decoding nature and recoding with human instruments to create new worlds means porous borders between forms of life and artifacts. When all is "information" on the one hand and "resources" on the other, as it is for the Information Revolution, the distinction between the organic and technical is leaky. It is not clear who makes and who is made in computer programs that can mutate, or what is mind and what is body in thinking machines. Nor is it altogether clear what is organ and what it not when a defective body part is replaced by a crafted one that performs the same function and is permanently attached to "other body parts." It even seems that the ontology of life and nature is no longer what it has always been. Anything and everything can be a matter of "systems" and "ecologies," and is. Everything can be "total" and "holistic" and simultaneously relative, mutable, and mobile. There are endless ways to "be" in a dynamic, relational mode. The decoded cannot only be recoded but transcoded as something which has not been. New life forms can be created and patented. Technology, like nature, is the rest of *us*, as it has always been. But the lines between technology and nature blur as never before.

If nature and technology are less discrete than ever, and borders more permeable, where is human power (and sustainability) in all this? When everything is susceptible to uncoding and all heterogeneity "can be submitted to disassembly, reassembly, investment, and exchange,"[73] then surely the last barriers have fallen to human power as instrumental control—the power of some humans more than others, to be sure. The world—all of it—is rendered a series of systemic problems and solutions. The people who count most, then, are those who understand systems and have access to information. All else is important, but as reduced to "resources." Power is "effective communication," whether the language is biology or engineering or both together.

Differently said, all the battles of long-standing Western dualisms of mind and matter, mind and body, human culture and resistant nature, have finally been resolved by this revolution. They have been resolved more successfully and unambiguously than the Industrial Revolution ever managed, in favor of human mind and culture as creators, controllers and high-tech cowboys working "integrated circuits" of various kinds. Relational, holistic, "ecological" thinking has thus triumphed in ways the Industrial Revolution never knew, as has decentralized networking as an organizational style working across distant "nodes." This is Western male-stream culture in a more "ecological" or "systems" mode but further from the rest of nature than before.

Peter Drucker thinks this is a massive social transformation in the making. Industrial society, he says, was still rather traditional in its basic social relationships of production. The society based on knowledge and knowledge workers is not. "It is the first society in which ordinary people—and that means most people—do not earn their daily bread by the sweat of their brow. It is the first society in which 'honest work' does not mean a callused hand. It is also the first society in which not everybody does the same work, as was the case when the huge majority were farmers or, as seemed likely only forty or thirty years ago, were going to be machine operators."[74] This is "far more than a social change," Drucker goes on. "It is a change in the human condition."[75]

That this is a change in the human condition is pondered further by Drucker. Information societies will be so mobile and dynamic that people will no longer have roots. They will not have neighborhoods and communities that do essential socialization. The welfare state and government was one go at this, "but it has been totally disproved"[76] as an effective agent of citizenship and moral formation. Drucker himself argued earlier, in The Future of Industrial Man (1942), that the big corporation should and could become the community successor to yesterday's village. The workplace would thus be the chief agent of socialization. He now scoffs at the notion. Some new social sector for "growing people up" (Richard Rohr) and creating human well-being is therefore necessary. We do not know what it is, concludes Drucker, we only know what it is not—business and government. And we know what the missing agent must do—recreate community.[77] But we do not know how it will do so. "Virtual community" via the Internet is not the answer.

Basically the problem is that in an information society of borderless networks and megaherz pace, no one is concerned with the common good and nothing steadily supplies the cohesion of society. So all Drucker sees emerging is a kind of "pluralism of feudalism." Private hands are assuming public power is a proliferation of fiefdoms.[78]

Drucker's insights on the social transformations of the Information Age are many. But he fails where most analysts do. He does not ask how the Information Revolution appears from the ground up, from the experience of earth, on which all utterly depends. And he does not ask what specific configurations human-earth relationships take in the wake of this revolution. He remains trapped in a "social" frame of mind, without realizing that all societies are configurations of nature that never break loose from impacting earth and being impacted by it. To see what Drucker's oversight means for sustainability and the play of human power, we must return to the earlier discussion of mind and matter, biology and information.

Information societies *try* to break loose from earth. "Information" here is largely disembodied content, the "codes" of things abstracted from all that makes the codes living flesh. Docetism flourishes here as "virtual reality." In fact, information as coded, recoded, transcoded reality carries a certain contempt for being earthbound at all. It prefers avoiding the messy world of finite, limited, placed, dependent bodies.

The information world may be, then, yet another revival of a certain Platonism in which immaterial pure forms inhabit another world as true "reality," while the flawed one we live in is the cave of shifting shadows. The earthbound is denigrated, the abstract and precisely mathematical are elevated and preferred. Important and formative reality travels the ether on a web of its own, unencumbered by the mundane material.

The docetism, furthermore, is married to another ancient heresy—gnosticism.[79] A saving *gnosis* (knowledge) rescues humankind from the damnable inconvenience of being trapped by earth's flawed creations. The *gnostikoi* (the priestly class of saving knowledge) stand apart from the *hoi polloi* and mediate saving knowledge to those who have ears to hear (i.e., are bright and educated and plugged in). What the priestly intellectual aristocrats offer, above all, is knowledge that meets the needs of the self as the emptiness and evil of the world become manifest. No *thing* matters to this knowledge elite, and creatures and their ways must not be confused with the truth. Creation is fundamentally flawed and stigmatized in this scheme, and a metaphysical alienation from earth is the beginning of wisdom itself. One is not saved by faith *in* God *in* creation, then. One's salvation is in knowledge that lets one escape earth's distress, along with concomitant responsibility for it. No one learns genuine compassion at a terminal.

This resolution of dysfunctional dualisms of mind and matter, body and spirit, mind and body, in favor of networks of disembodied "mind," information and a certain earth-avoiding spirit and ethic, will have as one certain outcome, then, the neglect of earth and those who inhabit its distress most directly. The material world beyond the information elites will grow shabbier as a consequence, and, in yet another instance of prophecy self-fulfilled, this will reinforce the contempt of information strata for the world. "Our material world gets dirtier . . . and more brutal as we go along," says one commentator. "So we're attracted to this etherial bill of goods we've been sold, this wonder world elsewhere."[80] Plato and *The Gospel of Truth*[81] live. Billions of poor people are simply not on the screen.

Perhaps little more need be said, in part because we are at an early stage of the Information Revolution and cannot assess a revolution which has not run its course. But for now the Information Revolution would seem both an intensification of industrial era logics and a new turn for them. It removes humanity yet further from its sense of embeddedness in nature and as part and parcel of it. It seems to treat all nature, humans included, in even more abstracted and utilitarian ways. All, without distinction, are "resources" and "capital." It further fosters the illusion that we control what we create and that what we can create knows no bounds. It does not place claims of its own on us, moral claims included. Through intensification of complex global systems, it appears as well to push the consequences of decisions still further from sight and thus dim down personal responsibility so as hardly to be felt in the gut at all. Not least, it further advantages the already advantaged and disadvantages the already dependent. And it intensifies the dynamics of a globalizing economy in ways that treat the planet as a commons for the taking, anywhere, anytime, night or day.

These are all extensions and intensifications of negative industrial era dynamics. No doubt the Information Revolution offers much that is positive and certainly much that is potentially of great significance and value. But the point here is not, in the first instance, a summary. It is to explain how we arrived at the state of *un*sustainability in a very crowded world and where and how we begin to wrest sustainability from present conditions. From such a vantage point, the promise and achievement of the Information Revolution is less apparent than is its part in aiding and abetting unsustainability by extending industrialism in new, more "efficient" and ecologically comprehensive ways. Some of it is *sheer* extension, simply a wider reach. So at the very first meeting of the G-7 countries (the United States, Japan, Britain, France, Germany, Italy, and Canada) after the conclusion of the seven-year GATT negotiations on trade and tariffs, the agenda turned chiefly to three areas not yet adequately covered by the *General Agreement on Trade and Tar-*

iffs: protecting "intellectual property" (patents, software, research, movies, videos); gaining more access for service industries such as insurance, banking, brokerage, and consulting; and lowering the barriers and securing more guarantees for the flow of billions of dollars (or yen, marks, or francs) of investment capital around the world and especially to emerging economies in Asia and Latin America.[82] All of these are quintessential "information revolution" industries, not "heavy" industry. Yet the economic dynamics and goals are the same. They are simply extended.

If there is a difference from industrialism, it is use of ecological or holistic thinking itself in the interests of colonization and conquest. Webs of information in earth-spanning networks in the hands of major economic players are the key.

Take present capitalism as an example of both an intensification of industrial-era dynamics and new twists and turns effected by the Information Revolution. Current capitalism has plural forms. The Europeans want to promote free markets vigorously, yet subordinate them to programs that place social welfare and regional interests above unfettered capitalism. The Americas, despite the Mexico fiasco, are, with the strong push and pull of the United States, pressing the agenda of deregulation and maximum feasible laissez-faire. The Asians continue to experiment with state capitalism, where government invests heavily in business enterprises and works consciously from detailed industrial policies for which government and business together are responsible.[83] At the same time, these different renditions of capitalism are all commonly affected by the Information Revolution. The engine seems to be "blitz capital," which can be moved anywhere anytime in what has become a twenty-four-hour planetary economy. There is more to it than rapidly moving capital, however. Despite the varieties of capitalism, the tendency is for fewer collective contracts, reduced power of unions and often of governments (except as allies for business), easy shifting of manufacturing to different regions, smaller size but coordinated establishments,

emphasis on short-term profitability over longer-term commitments and profitability, and less and less commitment
and attachment to people and place.[84] Capitalism has not
gone "postindustrial." But, with the help of the Information
Revolution, it has gone postmodern, aiding and abetting post-
modernity's fragmentation and relativization.

We might close this segment with a question: Precisely
what kind of knowing is it that we need? Is it "information,"
whether via the "information superhighway" or other
routes? Is a world of six billion dying for want of information? Is late twentieth-century life unsustainable because too
few data come our way and we just cannot get enough of that
wonderful stuff? Is it facts that we need but are not yet
known? While we certainly do need knowledge about the
empirical world, and while no truly integrated "earth science" of sustainability, population, and development yet
exists, the intuition runs deep that the issue is not knowledge so much as understanding and wisdom. The issue turns
not on more information but on the choices which ethics and
religion pose: What understanding do we need in order to live
with earth and one another, on terms enhancing for life in its
many guises? What sort of existence and way of life do we
need to learn so as to take responsibility for the home we
have? What norms and values do we measure information
itself by, as a source for what kind of society? These are not
questions for newborn gnostics and docetists. They are questions for plain earth creatures who know they have nowhere
else to go and whose (not wholly unhappy) destiny it is to
have been dumped on the beach at the end of the century by
the cresting waves of agricultural, industrial, and information revolutions.

SUSTAINABLE DEVELOPMENT OR
SUSTAINABLE COMMUNITY?

Sustainability, population, and development policy can
be approached through discussions of sustainable development. Many of these are heated discussions that only lightly

mask deep differences. The deliberations of international organizations such as the United Nations, the World Bank, the General Agreement on Tariffs and Trade (GATT) and World Trade Organization (WTO), and transnational corporations, arrayed on the one bank of the river, and nongovernmental organizations (NGOs) and peoples' movements, including resistance movements, on the other, compete with one another in the crowded scene this side of Sweet Betsy's avalanche. At issue are differing approaches to sustainability and how human power is socially configured. One approach understands sustainability as a crucial qualifier of development economics on a global scale. Development "qualifiers" or the "relaunchers" of development take this path. Another approach begins not with economics but ecology and not with a global reach but a local and regional one. This is the work of development "dissenters." Unraveling the knotty distinctions of "sustainable development" from "sustainable society" or "sustainable community" will be the agenda of the next pages. Conclusions for the whole then close this essay.

A vignette from the largest gathering of development agencies under one umbrella, the Society for International Development (SID), at its meeting in Mexico City in April, 1994, leads off. In the closing plenary on "Building Partnerships and Collaboration Towards Global Transformation," a representative of the indigenous peoples of the Mexican province of Chiapas was recognized. David Korten's account goes like this.

For the first and only time during the conference, we were hearing an authentic voice of the world's poor and marginalized, specifically a voice from a group that only a few months earlier had declared war on the Mexican government as an expression of its discontent. Without accusation or rancor, he spoke as a plain and simple man of the desire of his people to have the opportunity to free themselves from poverty. He spoke of foreign aid that had never reached the poor. He spoke of the love of his

people for the land, the trees, and the ocean. He spoke of
their desire to share their ideas as fellow human beings,
to have their existence recognized, to be accepted as
partners in Mexico's development. He spoke of the people's call for a new order in which they might find
democracy for all.[85]

Korten speaks of this as "a defining moment" in debates
about sustainable development because it bespoke a sharp
alternative to the conventional view. The Chiapas rebellion
was distinctive among guerrilla struggles in that it did not
seek to seize state power. Instead, *it aimed to win the right
of people to govern themselves within their own communities.* It did not call on other Mexicans to take up arms for a
new national social agenda, but for the space and means for
popular, democratic movements tied to particular locales.[86]
One commentator, Gustavo Esteva, called it "a new kind of
movement" and the "first revolution of the twenty-first century." By that he meant the feisty manifestation of a growing
struggle of people around the world for economic and political survival and sovereignty within their own communities.
This was not a Marxist guerrilla group. It had no clear-cut
ideology or political platform and no one leader. Nor was it a
fundamentalist or messianic group. Its members came from
different Indian groups, professed different religions, and
were explicitly ecumenical. As mentioned, its goal was *not to
seize power to govern the country,* but rather *to reclaim the
community.* It did not eshew, but instead used, modern
means of communication and a strategy of networking varied
coalitions of dissent. Most strikingly, it did not call on the
government for cheaper food, more jobs, more health care,
and more education. It was not, in Esteva's words, a revolt in
response to a *lack* of development (the list just enumerated)
but a response that Chiapas was being "developed to death."
People "opted for a more dignified way of dying."[87] A more
dignified way consisting of a "commons" the community
carves out for itself in response "to the crisis of development," "ways of living together that limit the economic

damage and give room for new forms of social life," and "life-support systems based on self-reliance and mutual help, informal networks for the direct exchange of goods, services and information," and "an administration of justice which calls for compensation more than punishment."[88] Esteva's conclusion is that the revolt was against conventional development as played out in Mexico. "To challenge the rhetoric of development, however, is not easy. Mexico's economic growth, the promise of prosperity tendered by the IMF and the World Bank, the massive investment in modernity as an integral element of the war against poverty—these have been cast as truths beyond question." Nonetheless, the Indian rebels "announced to the world that development as a social experiment has failed miserably in Chiapas."[89]

The background to this "announcement" is the following. Chiapas is among the richest of Mexico's provinces. It is endowed with a hundred thousand barrels of oil and five hundred billion cubic meters of gas per day; dams that supply better than half of Mexico's hydroelectric power; one third of the national production of coffee and a considerable percentage of the country's cattle, timber, honey, corn, and other products of the land. To connect these riches with the capital, a freeway is being built through the El Ocote forest to Mexico City.

Yet Chiapas is among the poorest of Mexico's provinces and a chief "target" of "Pronasol," the national war on poverty. One third of the population of 3.5 million is Indian. Large numbers of Indians have been displaced by dams, oil rigs, and cattle ranches, and have been pushed into the Selva Lacandona forest (the largest tropical forest in North America) where they have contended with loggers and ranchers. Thirty thousand Indians died in 1993 from hunger and disease, yet the entire social budget of Chiapas is a fraction of the cost of the freeway to Mexico City, despite the Prosonal.

The (now former) governor of Chiapas, Gonzalez Garrido, carried out a three-pronged program: he protected armed landowners and cattle raisers against Indian resistance to the taking of their lands, supported the creation of an Indian stratum to keep control of the villages, and gave free reign to the police in the name of combating drug trafficking. All this was called "modernization" and "development" and was highly lucrative for those who governed Chiapas and plied its economy. For his success, Garrido was appointed Mexican Minister of the Interior in 1993, part of recent successful economic growth generally in Mexico.[90]

The Zapatistas began their rebellion in January, 1994, two hours after the North American Free Trade Agreement (NAFTA) went into effect. Their appeals were, in Esteva's words, "for an end to five hundred years of oppression and forty years of 'development.'"[91]

Sharper contrasts could hardly be drawn between the Mexican Indian peoples' understanding of sustainable development and their government's program, the latter in partnership with transnational institutions. The contrasts can be summarized by saying that while conventional sustainable development revolves around economies and their growth in the form of free markets and economic globalization, the Indian notion of sustainability focuses on the health of communities and societies as tied to local self-reliance, social movements, culture, low-impact agriculture, sustainable energy use, environmental balance within locality and region, and community economic, social, and political accountability. Differently said and more broadly applied, *conventional sustainable development qualifies economic growth with a view to ecological sustainability while the alternative vision tries to increase local economic self-reliance within a framework of community responsibility and ecological balance.* The latter attention is to the webs of social relationships that define human community together with ecosystem webs and the regenerative capacities of both human and ecosystem communities, that is, sustainability. More starkly put, conventional development is globalization from above, as led by "developed" sectors around the world, the "Chiapas" alternative is globalization from below, led by "underdeveloped" sectors.[92] Or, in Nicholas Hildyard's telling distinction: local peoples' notion of sustainable development views the environment as "what is around their homes."

Government, business, and international organizations view the environment as "what is around their economies."[93]

This vignette and commentary are necessary to understanding the conflicts of North and South. As the global integration of economies progresses, power is shifting from both communities and nations to transnational capital and the institutions that wield and regulate it. Accompanying this is an increase in the gap between rich and poor both within and between nations and a parallel diminishing of local community power and oftentimes even national power to do much about it. Which is to say that *"North" and "South" are defined by class rather than geography.*

To be sure, "North" may still refer to nations in meaningful ways. After all, the preponderance of advanced industrial nations are in the northern hemisphere and wield great power as players in the globalized economy, with its notion of *sustainable economic growth on the capitalist model of liberalized international exchange.*

"South" may also refer to nations in part, but on the basis of whether they possess an "expanding frontier" or a "shrinking" one (the terms are Tariq Banuri's).[94] An expanding frontier means a nation judges that it has the wherewithal to successfully engage the global economy on competitive terms. It has expanding possibilities of growing income and wealth because it can command not just national but regional resources; that is, its economic frontier does not stop at its borders. It can "appropriate" carrying capacity from beyond its borders. Thailand, Malaysia, Singapore, and Indonesia all see themselves in this light, to use examples from Asia. A shrinking frontier belongs to those nations for whom a set of limitations on growth exists because of resource constraints and little leverage in a globalized economy. Pakistan has no more water and no more land and no significant access to world markets and prosperity. Bangladesh and, in a more complex way, even India, face shrinking rather than expanding frontiers, to continue Asian examples. Southern nations split along these lines now and assume different postures in treaty and trade debates hammering out the terms of sustainable development.

All this noted, the more salient fact nonetheless is that "North" now stands for classes everywhere in the world who are aligned with transnational capital and who see their own welfare or demise tied to the success or failure of the world economy. "South" designates those, whether they be in New York, Mexico City, Lagos, or Ankara, who are pressed more and more toward the margins in the globalization process. Oftentimes this means, as in the case of indigenous peoples and subsistence farmers, seeing their land appropriated for export-driven agriculture with little attention given to either their own regenerative needs or the land's. And it means, for blue-and white-collar workers and the unemployed of urban megapolises, highly mobile capital and not-as-mobile labor, accompanied by depressed wages, corporations shedding workers, and people displaced from their homes and means of livelihoods. In all cases, it means the stark absence of attention to the essential importance of *a healthy* spiritual *connection to nature, place, community and culture.* (This absence is somewhere near the heart of the Chiapas quest for an alternative.)

In sum, North and South correlate less with geography than with those who, on the one hand, pursue sustainable development in tandem with growth-driven economies as part and parcel of a globally integrated economy and those who, on the other, grope for a local alternative.[95] Or, in terms used at the outset, the divide between the development qualifiers (sustained economic growth within sustained environments) and development dissenters (global schemes rejected in favor of local and regional alternatives that deplete neither local communities nor ecosystems).[96] Not by accident, globalization-oriented leadership is overwhelmingly male, community-oriented leadership both male and female.

In the end, the prestigious Brundtland Report, prepared for the Earth Summit, probably best reflects where dominant thinking and practice is on sustainability and sustainable development. It documents clearly and forcefully the devastation of the environment at human hands. It singles out the limited capacity of nature to continue absorbing the waste products of world energy consumption and shows how economic growth has been deleterious toward the same resources on which it is dependent. It records the brutal statistics of wasteful overconsumption in some quarters and crushing poverty in others. It casts its eye to the welfare of future generations and warns the present about the deprivations it is creating for them. It faces the realities of exploding populations head on. On the prescriptive side, it calls for major reductions in arms expenditures as well as major reductions in its chief target, poverty. It commends multilateral cooperation on all these border-crossing problems and, together with the Business Council for Sustainable Development, says that sustainability demands attention to the entire life cycle of goods and requires the internalizing of all costs in production, distribution, and consumption, including environmental ones all along the way. In short, it shows a possible path for continuing development and rendering it sustainable.[97]

But after all this, which is purported to challenge radically standard development thought and practice, *Our Common Future* goes on to say, first, that "if large parts of the developing world are to avert economic, social, and environmental catastrophes, it is essential that global economic growth be revitalized";[98] and then, in its key recommendations, calls for global economic growth at a level five to ten times the current output! Furthermore, the stimulus for this is increased consumption in the North since greater Northern consumption will create greater demand for Southern products.[99] This is oddly askew of the earlier analysis, where growth and consumption are the problem. Now they are suddenly a considerable segment of the solution. Or, to nuance this in the way Brundtland does: more ecoefficient production, distribution and consumption, along with social changes, will render the necessary five- to tenfold economic increase ecologically benign.

One can only sympathize with Brundtland. A bulging world cannot develop in a way that meets basic, escalating needs without relying substantially on economic growth. Chances for meeting exploding needs while suffering declining national incomes are slim, by any standards. Yet how growth-driven economies are made compatible with biospheric sustainability in a world where the scale of human activity relative to the biosphere is already much too large is anything but clear—and may be impossible.

In a word, sustainable development on this scheme simply bundles contradictions without resolving them or showing the way forward, a judgment now dawning on those working with *Agenda 21*, the United Nations' master plan for sustainable development signed by all heads of state at the Earth Summit. There is even a sense of desperation here, though it is usually cast, cheerleader fashion, as the next great challenge. Stephen Schmidheiny, Chairman of the Business Council for Sustainable Development, was interviewed by *Neue Züricher Zeitung* in December, 1990, and confronted with the statistical likelihood (read: *un*likelihood) of successfully combining economic growth and environmental protection on the necessary scale. "Isn't this combination just a dream?" the reporter asked. "It brings together things that don't match." Schmidheiny replied, "For the time being, that's true,"[100] and went on to issue the call to find ways to refute this truth as an enduring one.

All that is imperative for the remainder of this discussion is understanding whence sustainable development came. Key here is the development of "development" itself, since it remains the noun; "sustainable" is a modifier.

DEVELOPMENT'S HISTORY

In his Inaugural Address as President of the United States in 1949, Harry Truman spoke of "a major turning point in the long history of the human race."[101] With fascism defeated, the world's chance for democratic freedom and prosperity had arrived. In the interests of this freedom, Truman offered a "bold new program for making the benefits of our scientific advances and industrial progress available for the improvement and growth of underdeveloped areas."[102]

This designation—underdeveloped areas—soon became standard vocabulary. Distinctions were drawn between "developed" and "underdeveloped" nations, with "developed" a clear-cut notion and the telos for the "underdeveloped" world. Truman had himself supplied the criterion in his Inaugural for moving from an underdeveloped to developed condition: "Greater production is the key to prosperity and peace." He went on to explain that "the key to greater production is a wider and more vigorous application of modern scientific and technical knowledge." "The United States," he noted, "is preeminent among nations in the development of industrial and scientific techniques."[103]

Later the terms would modulate somewhat to "developed" and "developing," but the model remained the same: *development meant the way of life of capitalist democracies as defined by modern economic progress and advanced science and technology.* Wolfgang Sachs, writing in 1992 about the roots of development, sums up the legacy from 1949 onward as follows: "The degree of civilization in a country could from now on be measured by its level of production. This new concept allowed the thousands of cultures to be separated into the two simple categories of 'developed' and 'underdeveloped.' Diverse societies were placed on a single progressive track, more or less advancing according to the criteria of production."[104] Developing countries were junior versions of developed ones; developed ones were affluent industrialized democracies.

Of course, from another slant there is little "new" in this "new concept." It remains essentially the nineteenth-century European and American one of successful industrialism: higher levels of material consumption and a heightened ability to alter the natural world for human benefit hold the key to progress. Progress is by definition beneficial, something all societies should shoot for, and associated most of all with economic growth and democracy.[105] If there is something new here, it is the application of these postwar distinctions of "developed" and "developing," or "more developed" and "less developed," to all societies everywhere.

Our attention, however, is also to the notion of sustainability which now accompanies this understanding of development. Initially a strictly economic one, presented among other places in W. W. Rostow's widely used *Stages of Economic Growth*, sustainability meant the critical threshold over which an economy passes so as to enter *long-term, continuous growth*.[106] To this day, and for all but an (increasing) few, development is quite unimaginable apart from sustained growth, even when "sustainability" is no longer a narrowly economic notion. "Sustainable" has now come to mean rising national incomes *together with* environmental preservation. (Both the Brundtland report, *Our Common Future*, and the U.N. master plan, *Agenda 21*, define it this way.) Sustainability is essentially, then, *sustainable economic growth* in a double sense: ongoing or "sustained" production to meet expanded human wants and needs (the Truman-Rostow notion of sustainability) *and* production that nature can sustain (the Earth Summit's crucial qualification). In some ways this means great change. Talk of "paradigm shifts" and a "second industrial revolution of ecoefficiency" is the language used by Stephan Schmidheiny, the Swiss businessman and millionaire who organized the Business Council for Sustainable Development. "The single biggest problem" within "the larger challenge of sustainable development," Schmidheiny says, is the requirement "for clean, equitable economic growth everywhere."[107]

"Clean, equitable economic growth everywhere" would indeed be a paradigm shift, especially "clean" and "equitable" "everywhere"!

In any case, the focus of sustainability in this view, with paradigms shifting or not, is on *economies and their growth*. This rests in three tenets David Korten calls the "modern theology" of development: (1) sustained economic growth is both possible and the key to human progress; (2) integration of the global economy is the key to growth and beneficial to all but a few narrow special interests; and (3) international assistance and foreign investment are important contributors to alleviating poverty and protecting the environment.[108]

This may sound attractive enough, conventional enough, or perhaps simply banal enough, to garner broad consensus. But it did not. In fact the Chiapas Zapatistas came to be true disbelievers. They rejected this faith and its promises. Still, our purpose at this point is not to record and judge the reception of sustainable development so much as trace approaches to sustainability and how it is to be realized, given the planet's exploding human numbers. And what has been sketched thus far, to sum up, is the history of sustainability on the part of those *who begin with the massively institutionalized means of development regnant since the end of World War II and who move from there to qualify this now global apparatus in a way that renders both growth and the biosphere "sustainable."*

While this is clearly the dominant approach to sustainability and the reigning notion of sustainable development, we note the other approach. The Chiapas rebellion was a glimpse. But it says too little. It says too little because the sources of this alternative approach include not only the long history of resistance to Western-instituted globalization and the invasionary power of the Neo-Europes. The sources include established and growing middle-income ranks far from marginalized peoples. Many of the established affluent, too, are now convinced the current economic course is simply unsustainable, even when environmentally sensitized. What these varied sources hold in common is *a reverse ordering of economy and ecology*. The issue for many in both North and South (used now in a geographical sense) is *not how to alter environments so as to serve the economy and yet be sustained, but how to alter economies so as to serve comprehensive environments*. The difference is not subtle. Against the background of two centuries of industrial economies, it is the difference between an economic approach which begins with a notion of an "open," even "empty" and basically unlimited world, and an ecological approach which begins with a notion of a "full" and limited world that can only operate on a principle of borrowing. It is the difference of a mobile world (including mobile homes!) and a world of place and roots. It is the difference between viewing the whole world as sets of industrial and information "systems" that need to be "managed" globally as "human" and "natural" "capital," and local and regional communities attending to home environments in a comprehensive way around basic needs and "quality of life." It is the difference between saving the planet and saving the neighborhood. The former asks the kind of pretentious questions *Scientific American* did in its issue on "Managing the Planet," the latter does not pretend such reach or assume such a posture.

> Two central questions must be addressed: What kind of planet do we want? What kind of planet can we get? . . . How much species diversity should be maintained in the world? Should the size or the growth rate of the human population be curtailed . . . ? How much climate change is acceptable?[109]

Community sustainability asks less totalistic questions. Not "singular man" facing "singular nature" (Raymond Williams) but questions more soul-sized and from a very different place, a place more familiar as home earth and less gnostic and docetic.

MORAL NORMS AND POLICY

Policy for this next journey of somehow achieving sustainability and development for an earth community of six billion and more is daunting! A modesty forced by circumstances and the enduring power of a long history of unsustainable, but still institutionalized, developments allows only the barest confidence about where to go from here. But the direction seems something like the following.

The threat to a sustainable world arises both from "overgrazing" in the manner of the present flat-earth, cowboy economy of global capitalism and from the illusions of those who would offer planetary management. (A negative example from *Scientific American* again: "Self-conscious, intelligent management of the earth is one of the great challenges facing humanity as it approaches the twenty-first century."]¹¹⁰ After all, it is not so much the planet that has gone haywire or lacks intelligently developed resources, but us. Wrongheaded notions, human numbers, greed and vast over-consumption by the billion most well-off, arrogance, ignorance, prejudice, stupidity, and the three great instabilities of injustice, unpeace, and the disintegration of creation at human hands are what most needs to be taken into account. And they are not much given to cure by technical prowess, globalizing capitalism, or planetary management, spaceship style. Human dreaming and imagination are certainly needed, but as wed to ecumenical moral sensibilities and the religious conviction that life so often makes its most startling appearances amid conditions smelling of death.

The moral sensibilities and stimuli for hope are crucial. For policy they underline issues of participation and accountability: who gets to sit at the policy tables, whose knowledge and experience count, who casts what kind of votes, who represents future generations and those of the present who cannot speak for themselves, whose values and character carry the day. These questions are vital because "sustainable" modifies both "environment" and "society" and both together at once. Both are dynamic processes without foreseen ends, processes that depend heavily on human constructs of both heart and mind, and, to use World Council of Churches' language, some modicum of "justice, peace and the integrity of creation."

Against the long foregoing narrative, one might, then, offer these as the moral norms for policy formulation, realizing that sound moral norms are only one element of good policy.

Participation as the optimal inclusion of all involved voices in society's decisions and in obtaining and enjoying the benefits of society and nature, together with sharing their burdens. To date the populations most obvious among the missing are women around the world, the poor and minorities in most societies, and indigenous peoples.

Sufficiency as the commitment to meet the basic material needs of all life possible. This means sufficiency for both human and otherkind's populations. For humans it means careful organization of the economics of borrowing and sharing, requiring both floors and ceilings for consumption. It thus means that a sufficiency revolution must accompany the much-lauded "second industrial revolution of ecoefficiency" called for by the United Nations and sensitive sectors of the business community.

Accountability as the sense and structuring of responsibility toward one another and earth itself, carried out in ways that prize openness or "transparency." (Accountability is sometimes considered a dimension of participation but here the character of that participation is made clear.)

Material simplicity and spiritual richness as markers of a quality of life that includes bread for all (i.e., sufficiency) but is more than bread alone. Negatively stated, major disparities of wealth and poverty generate instability and unsustainability. So do soul-barren cultures that substitute higher levels of material consumption for more appropriate ways of meeting the needs of the spirit.

Responsibility on a *scale* that people can handle. This is an argument for actions commensurate with workable community (rather than unworkable "global consciousness"). It is also an argument for technologies whose consequences are more apparent rather than less, are smaller in their range of impact than larger, and are subject to alteration and correction without vast disruption.[111]

These may suffice as moral norms for policy orientation and formulation. But they do not yet suggest process and scale for policy. To that end, we draw from a process norm with a long history in Christian ethics, one especially attuned to the community scale this essay promotes as the proper way to relate sustainability, population, and production-consumption. That process norm is subsidiarity. Subsidiarity is the means of participation and accountability best aligned to the pluralism of place and the scale most likely to be responsible. We consider it in some detail.

One of the more recent formulations of subsidiarity is a papal one: "Just as it is gravely wrong to take from individuals what they can accomplish by their own initiative and industry and give it to the community, so also it is an injustice and at the same time a grave evil and disturbance of right order to assign to a greater and higher association what lesser and subordinate organizations can do."[112] Translated, this means that what can be accomplished on a smaller scale at close range by high participation with available resources should not be given over to, or allowed to be taken over by, larger and more distant organizations. Do not transfer to supposedly "higher" and larger collectivities what can be provided and performed by (allegedly) "lesser" and "subordinate" ones.

The key is *appropriate* scale and action. For sustainable community, that may in fact mean actions, policies and institutions that are *more global*. Rectifying ozone damage or reducing greenhouse gases means international treaties with authority ceded from local and regional bodies, for example. Massive waves of refugees and internally displaced persons also require broader response than local resources can provide. The protection of marine ecosystems and fish populations cannot be done without transnational cooperation. Nor can much pollution control, or other threats to a shared atmosphere. Oceans, genetic diversity, climate, the ozone layer, and even forests and other great concentrations of green plant matter form a kind of global commons that must be treated as such. In a small and contracting world, global community requires some institutions and policies with genuinely global reach.

But subsidiarity also means massively deconstructing what is now globalized. Food, shelter, livelihood, and other needs which can be met on a community and regional basis, with indigenous resources, talent, and wisdom, should be met there, with firm commitments to pluralism of place. Even large cities can better relate to the bioregions in which they and surrounding areas are embedded. Vancouver is not Rio, despite the presence of striking mountains and sea for both.

Most of the other explicit norms for sustainable community—participation, solidarity, sufficiency, material simplicity, spiritual richness, responsibility, and accountability—are also better served when subsidiarity is heeded. If converting linear processes (the industrial paradigm) to cyclical and spiral ones (nature's economy) is one key to sustainability, making "feedback" visible and close to home is another. Local and regional initiative and self-reliance tend to promote these, just as they tend to promote higher degrees of cooperation, mutual support, and collaborative problem-solving. Not least, subsidiarity tends to preserve resources in the community as the "commons"[113] people depend on, know best, and care most about.

Stephen Viederman gives particular emphasis to the role of human imagination and collaboration in arriving at sustainable community. That, too, is best served by subsidiarity. Viederman finds the transition to sustainability under present and foreseeable conditions fraught with staggering operational problems. Making the transition from present unsustainability to future sustainability cannot, he is certain, be well addressed either by comprehensive planning or the roulette of the market. "The first task" of sustainability, then, is "to provide the space and time for people to begin to envision the future they desire for their [own] communities, and to ensure access to power that will make it happen."[114] That "first task" is more likely accomplished on the scale for which subsidiarity is the guide.

An example of Viederman's point is the case of the Environmental Protection Agency (EPA) of the U.S. government under the leadership of William Ruckelshaus. Under the Clean Air Act of 1970, the EPA had the authority to decide the fate of a smelting plant that was both a major polluter and a major employer in Tacoma, Washington (the annual payroll was $23 million). The issues were thus jobs, the local economy, and health. Instead of making the decision in Washington, D.C., Ruckelshaus took the matter to Tacoma. And there, instead of setting up only the required public hearings, he and other local officials initiated a series of public work-shops. These included plant workers, union representatives, local citizen participation, and environmental groups. The same format was used for all meetings. It included education about plant emissions, incidences of disease, local economic implications of possible courses of actions, and so on, as well as time for prepared testimony and open deliberation. What the community eventually decided was not in the minds of Ruckelshaus, local EPA officials, or the citizens themselves when the process began. The collective decision was that Tacoma's economy needed to diversify and there were ways to do that, ways that included retraining present plant work-ers. The community together had found a way to recast the "keep-the-plant-open-or-close-it" issue and decide what they wanted for their community. Ruckelshaus's later reflection on the process included a line from Thomas Jefferson: "If we think (the people) not enlightened enough to exercise their control with a wholesome discretion, the remedy is not to take it from them, but to inform their discretion." It was a lesson in leadership, community process, and imagination.[115]

Yet even this example of subsidiarity does not mean slavish localism as the standard, since subsidiarity asks not for the most local, but the most appropriate level of organi-zation and response. "Most appropriate" includes the *morally* most appropriate level. Small *as* beautiful, and the local as the *basic* unit of the global, may locate the starting blocks, in Tacoma as elsewhere. But in a world of maldistrib-uted resources and power, the local cannot be the only locus of responsible action, just as it is not the only place we meet and live together. Trade and other exchanges of resources, for example, are as necessary in their own way as is transna-tional cooperation to address global warming and regions suf-fering "overshoot" of their carrying capacity. The necessary guideline is not "no trade" or "no markets," or even "mini-mal trade" and "minimal markets." The guideline is to min-imize the *appropriation* of carrying capacity *from elsewhere*, thus risking other people's and otherkind's lives in the pre-sent and for the future. The guideline is also *restoration* of diminished carrying capacity and the empowerment of peoples whose resources have been diminished as a systemic feature of the globalizing dynamics of Western-led development. What is *not* in view is the plantation and colony economics of "the big house" and a sea of shacks, with its savage inequalities, as the shape of local household and habitat.

If there is something that should be added to past accounts of subsidiarity, it is lessons from listening to nature itself.

Sustainability guided by subsidiarity betters its chances, for example, by incorporating nature's resiliency into social systems. The practices of economy and society ought to be ordered in such a way as to be able to shift and adapt, like nature, to changing conditions. In nature, biodiversity is the mechanism by which adaptation to demanding changes occurs, the means by which nature is resilient in the face of often traumatic change. As such, it is the basic source of all future wealth and well-being.[116]

Paul Hawken's two principles of good social design, drawn from nature, would improve the odds in favor of greater resiliency. Good design "changes the least number of elements to achieve the greatest result." In Morocco, a 10 kilowatt wind turbine, which would only supply one American home with electric heat, pumps drinking water for a village of four thousand.[117] And good design "removes stress from a system rather than adding it."[118] Mexico's first wind farm emerged as part of an energy strategy to avoid paying $3.2 million for an electric power line in the Yucatan.[119] In short, easier and simpler is better. Easier and simpler, with room for error, favors sustainability.

The return to how nature works is an apt reminder that sustainability, and thus subsidiarity, necessarily involves the total earth-human process. It encompasses the requirements of sustainable environments, societies, livelihoods, economies, and ways of life. These *must function as a phase of earth economics and community.* Creation as a community remains the first stipulation, just as the integrity of ecosystems remains the first value.

IN SUM

We do not lack examples of actions and policy direction appropriate to sustainable community. A running list can easily be offered. In New York City, Bernadette Kosar's Greening of Harlem project targets environmental and social needs in the same action. She gathers Harlem teenagers to reclaim vacant lots and portions of school grounds as neighborhood and school gardens. The project has attracted the participation of the elderly as well as children, and come to include the support of nonprofit groups of all kinds. Kosar sees jobs in this movement as well, just as she sees "growing everything from food to herbs, everything from dyes to potpourris and tomato preserves."[120] Yet her larger point is the evolution of a healthier community on a scale that includes high levels of local particpation and pride and often a change of collective character itself. "Nature doesn't make people wild, it doesn't make people uncivilized," she says. "But I think concrete, asphalt, and steel does. It makes people hard, it makes people cold, it makes people inhuman. We have to figure a way to bring nature back to our cities."[121] In Costa Rica, a dozen peasant farmers came together in 1988 to form the San Miguel Association for Conservation and Development (ASACODE). This was their attempt to keep local forests under the control of local communities. They managed to find incentives for local people to harvest and process wood sustainably and develop regional markets for their products. In a country with Central America's highest rate of deforestation at the hands of big companies that have been buying out small local landowners, this was a turnaround. ASACODE has since developed nursuries for native tree stock and educated neighboring villagers in sustainable forestry.[122] The Deccan Development Society of Andhra Pradesh, India, organizes *sangams*, communities of women in villages that work toward gender equity, establish credit programs, cultivate and use medicinal herbs, incorporate organic gardening techniques and multiple cropping into local agricultural practices, and plant trees.[123] The Land

Resource Management on the Central Plateau in Burkina Faso (PATECORE) has found a way for two hundred forty marginal villages to transform ten thousand hectares of previously unproductive drylands in such a manner that the previous average family food deficit of 645 kilograms per year has turned into a 150 kilogram surplus. The key was combining systematic agricultural surveys with a process by which villagers covered the area with miniature dams and embankments and other small-scale irrigation devices they designed themselves, together with manure composting units they designed in order to fertilize previously unfertilized crops.[124] On a different scale and working other areas, Japan's Ministry of International Trade and Industry established an Institute of Innovative Technology with the explicit purpose of "undo[ing] the damage done to the earth over the past two centuries, since the industrial revolution." The Institute is exploring alternatives to chloroflurocarbons (CFCs) and trying to develop biodegradable plastics, hydrogen-producing bacteria, carbon-dioxide scrubbers, and genetically engineered algae for higher efficiency photosynthesis. In Germany the Federal Association for Ecologically Conscious Management is developing integrated management systems in accord with six principles: quality throughout the life cycle of a product; a creative work force enhanced by a friendly environment that focuses on low noise, healthy food, good air quality, and ecologically oriented architecture and furnishings; employee morale, which improves when corporate goals include both environmental well-being and economics; profitability as increased by adopting cost-reducing ecological innovations and marketing environmentally friendly products; continuity and security understood as avoiding environmental liability risks as well as market risks from decreasing demand for damaging products; and loyalty, built up when employees believe in their company's goals.[125] Germany's "take-back" legislation is still another large-scale example of widespread applicability. Industries are, in effect, forced to use life-cycle analysis in design and production of their goods since products must easily be converted into

future raw materials and their components have to be non-
toxic to worker exposure. The legislation also tends to end
planned obsolescence because increased product life is more
cost effective than constant collection and recycling.[126] The
Emilia-Romagna district of northern Italy has added important considerations of scale to earth-friendly manufacturing.
The results are astounding. Over twenty-five years, decentralized "flexible manufacturing networks" have created
twenty thousand new jobs, wage rates 175 percent above the
Italian average, and a step-up from seventeenth in 1970 to
second in 1995 in per-capita income among Italy's twenty-
one regions. These results were achieved chiefly by changing
the size and shape of manufacturing. Now the region has
more than 325,000 small firms, 90,000 of them in manufacturing. 90 percent of these firms employ fewer than twenty-
two persons each with most manufacturing firms employing
fewer than five persons. At the same time each tiny company
can draw on a large regional pool of highly trained artisans
who have developed impressive technologies and can use the
services of trade associations designed to keep the region's
companies competitive. David Wann sums up the goals and
norms of these varied efforts as "renewability, reversibility,
equity, resilience, proximity, and precision."[127] It takes only a
moment's reflection to recognize these as traits of sustainable community itself.

We do not lack examples, then. What we lack are the
collective mind-set and policies that routinely institutional-
ize the basic principles of ecological design. These in place,
our examples and more would quickly multiply as a critical
mass. The general principles, crisply put, are as follows:

- "Solutions grow from place." What does nature permit in a
  given locale, and What does it help us do? are the right
  questions to pose for this attention to specific site possibilities and limitations. "Without the details nothing can be
  known, not a lily or a child," writes Diane Ackerman.[128]
- "Ecological accounting informs design." Just as a full
  accounting of economic costs is a matter of conventional

design now, so must a full accounting of ecological costs be, from resource depletion to pollution and habitat destruction to disposal and reuse.

- "Design with nature." "Cradle-to-cradle" design, rather than "cradle-to-grave," is the going norm. What is waste for one species becomes food and habitat and resources for another.
- "Everyone is a designer." Good designs grow and evolve organically out of a process of communication that includes widespread and varied participation.
- "Make nature visible." What van der Ryn and Cowan call "flush and forget" technologies do not build a sense of responsibility or nurture earth-oriented mindfulness. Awareness of biological and other consequences of our actions by keeping them in view and acting back on us at shorter range rather than longer fosters responsibility and accountability.[129]

Were we to incorporate these principles into a summary of this entire essay, the results would essentially be David Orr's four-things-always-to-keep-in-mind for the transition to sustainable community.

First, people are finite and fallible. Our capacity to understand complexity and scale, much less manage it, is limited. Things too big are a liability.

Second, a sustainable world can only be put together from the bottom up. The building units are communities, and communities of communities. The social capital of smaller networks enabling larger ones is critical. Avoid the elitism and imperial reach of "planetary management."

Third, the crucial knowledge is knowledge that co-evolves from culture and nature together in a given locale (remembering that "locale" in a world full of life and under house arrest has different dimensions, from an immediate neighborhood to the oceans and the atmosphere).

Lastly, the true harvest for ongoing evolution is embedded in nature's own designs. Nature is not first of all a big bank of resources standing at the ready, it is the source and model for the very designs we must draw on in order to address the problems we face. Our design epistemologies must be compatible with the rest of nature's.[130]

Is this enough? Maybe. Yet not unless there is a human energy and disposition that helps make all this possible. Sustainable community will not happen apart from some source of renewable moral-spiritual vigor.

Faith is the name of the strong power serving as the source of moral-spiritual vigor. It squarely faces the fact there will never be decisive proof beforehand that life will triumph. Yet it still acts with confidence that the stronger powers in the universe arch in the direction of sustaining life, as they also insist on justice. Worldweariness is combatted by a surprising force found *amidst* earth and its distress. Creation carries its own hidden powers. It supports the confidence of the gospel that a steadfast order exists which bends in the direction of life and gives it meaning.

Said differently, the religious consciousness and dream that generates hope and a zest and energy *for* life is tapped *in* life itself. The finite bears the infinite, the transcendent is as close as the neighbor, soil, air, and sunshine itself. God, like the devil and life itself, is in the details. A turn to earth is thus also a turn to those sources that enable what has not yet come to pass to do so.

We have all been raised on a mess of stories, including faith in progress itself. Many of those stories no longer lead where we must go. But, with some of those stories and others not yet told, we will write our own. As we do so we will learn that faith is the great confronter, uncovering in us a capacity to fight for life in the face of death and venture the risks necessary to be part of a radically changed world. We will also learn, paradoxically, that faith is the great *unknowing*, the experience of an active mystery that surpasses all our words for it and leaves us with either silence or song, without pretension, and accepting, without despair, the tragic limitations of the human condition. The great unknowing is also the experience of a finitude that crushes any remaining homocentrism and exposes all our efforts to know *the* truth as self-deceptive. Our understandings are provisional and tentative, small little children of small times and places we are privileged to share. They are also in glorious degree part of the community of creation that includes and transcends us. Yet precisely here it is not we alone but—to put it in necessarily limited human terms—the *entire* community of creation that "knows" and remembers and learns and evolves and creates, from the cell to the galaxy and beyond. Faith has ears for such stories, and warns against mistaking human maps for the territory itself. Mistaking maps for territory is the culprit that turns limited human knowledge into imperial rule and destructive efforts to get a controlling grip on reality. Better to join the solidarity of the shattered and have ears to heart the stories of a compassionate Presence in league with those humble enough to know they are not less than, or more than, frail, beautiful children of the universe.

Such is the disposition for the task at hand, the fashioning of sustainable community on a small planet.

NOTES

1. William Stevens, Review of *Mortgaging the Earth: The World Bank, Environmental Impoverishment, and the Crisis of Development,* by Bruce Rich, *New York Times,* 6 March 1994, sec. 7, p. 29.

2. Ibid.

3. Ibid.

4. Alfred W. Crosby, *Ecological Imperialism: The Biological Expansion of Europe, 900–1900* (Cambridge: Cambridge University Press, 1986), n.p., citing Adam Smith, *The Wealth of Nations.*

5. Ibid.

6. Ibid., 2.

7. Ibid., 3.

8. Ibid., 302–303.

9. Ibid., 5.

10. Ibid., 303.

11. Ibid.

12. Ibid., 11.

13. Ibid., 6–7.

14. Ibid., 7.

15. See Timothy C. Weiskel, "In Dust and Ashes: The Environmental Crisis in Religious Perspective," *Harvard Divinity Bulletin* 21, no. 3 (1992): 8.

16. Ibid., 11.

17. Ibid. Much of the controversy at the Rio Earth Summit was over principles and treaties which create or retain access by firms and nations chiefly of the North to tropical forests and their lode of treasures, including biodiversity.

18. Crosby, 131.

19. On a personal note and for purposes of illustration, I report a moment during a visit in Larnaca, Cyprus, for a World Council of Churches meeting. Cyprus, with nine thousand years of continuous human habitation, has a sixteenth-century English cemetery. One tombstone reads: "Mary the wife of Samuel Palmer Died the 15th of July 1720 and Here Lies Buried With Her Infant Daughter." What were the English doing in Cyprus in 1720? What were they doing there when times were tough and dangers abundant, like Mary Palmer dying with her child? Why this mass movement to foreign parts, often deadly ones for aliens as well as native inhabitants? Mary Palmer of Larnaca is but a glimpse into Crosby's biological and ecological expansion of Europe.

20. Donna Haraway, *Primate Visions: Gender, Race, and Nature in the World of Modern Science* (New York: Routledge, 1989), 289.

21. Crosby, 131.

22. Ibid.

23. Maria Mies and Vandana Shiva, *Ecofeminism* (London: Zed Books, 1993), 32.

24. Crosby, 208–209.

25. Ibid.

26. The Declaration of Independence is without doubt one of the great documents of ethics and liberty in human history. Its effort to express the cosmopolitan ethic of Enlightenment universalism, and consider "all men" as "created equal" and "endowed by their Creator with certain inalienable Rights," is nonetheless part of a larger mind-set and cosmology that betrays its universalism in favor of the missionary cause of European civilization. One of the Declaration's complaints against King George himself is that he "has endeavored to bring on the inhabitants of our frontiers, the merciless Indian Savages, whose known rule of warfare is an undistinguished destruction of all ages, sexes and conditions." Quoted from Henry Steele Commager and Richard B. Morris, *The Spirit of 'Seventy-Six* (New York: Harper & Row, 1958), 319. The irony of which peoples most suffered "an undistinguished destruction of all ages, sexes, and conditions" should not escape us, as noted in Crosby's citation from Charles Darwin about the fate of indigenous peoples.

27. Weiskel, 10.

28. Ibid.

29. Ibid.

30. Crosby, 193–194.

31. National Round Table on the Environment and the Economy, "The Challenge," in *1991–92 Annual Review* (Ottawa: National Round Table Secretariat, 1992), 4.

32. Daniel Maguire, *The Moral Core of Judaism and Christianity: Reclaiming the Revolution* (Minneapolis: Fortress Press, 1993), 13.

33. "The Challenge," 4.

34. In addition to the Canadian materials, see Gerald O. Barney with Jane Blewett and Kristen R. Barney, *Global 2000 Revisited: What Shall We Do?* (Arlington, VA: Public Interest Publications, 1993). This important volume of the challenges for the next generations effectively uses graphs with an overlay of the lifetime of a child born in the 1990s.

35. Clive Ponting, *A Green History of the World: The Environment and the Collapse of Great Civilizations* (New York: Penguin Books, 1991), 52. On change and relocation, recall the "biological expansion" and "ecological imperialism" of the Neo-Europes.

36. A fuller account is available in many places. Among these the reader can consult Brian Swimme and Thomas Berry, *The Universe Story* (San Francisco: Harper San Francisco, 1992), especially 173–181; Ponting, *A Green History of the World*, especially, 37–67; and Crosby, *Ecological Imperialism*, especially 8–40. I have used a brief composite of these sources.

37. "First Settlers Domesticated Pigs Before Crops," *New York Times*, 31 May 1994, sec. C, p. 6.

38. See "Find Suggests Weaving Preceded Settled Life," *New York Times*, 9 May 1995, sec. C, pp. 1, 10.

39. Ponting, 64–65.

40. Ibid., 65.

41. Ibid., 66.

42. Shemaya Ben-David, *Megiddo Armageddon* (Privately printed, 1979), 1.

43. Ponting, 67.

44. Crosby, 32.

45. See especially William H. McNeill, *Plagues and Peoples* (Garden City, N.Y.: Anchor Doubleday, 1976); but also his related work, *The Human Condition: An Ecological and Historical View* (Princeton, NJ: Princeton University Press, 1980).

46. As cited in Paul Hawken, *The Ecology of Commerce* (New York: Harper Business, 1993), 7.

47. Ponting, 396.

48. Peter Drucker, "The Age of Social Transformations," *The Atlantic Monthly*, November 1994, 59.

49. Ponting, 394.

50. Hawken, 130.

51. Wendell Berry, "Does Community Have a Value?" Chap. in *Home Economics* (San Francisco: North Point Press, 1987), 179.

52. Hawken, 21–22.

53. Ponting, 396–407.

54. G. Whit Hutchinson's discussion of this way of understanding by way of investigating key words adds other light. "Theory" is from the Greek *theoros*, meaning "spectator." We regard what we know, then, as "out there," exterior to us, perhaps on stage. If we are drawn into it unduly, we would lose our perspective as spectator and no longer be "objective." And claims which are not "objective" are a species of prejudice or passion. Furthermore, the Latin and German of "objective" mean to "stand over against" and "to put against" or "oppose," with the connotation that knowledge is there to order reality outside us. "Reality" itself is from the Latin, *res*, meaning property, possession, a thing (thus "real estate"). Reality is something we lay claim on, own, perhaps even possess and control as spectators. See G. Whit Hutchinson, "The Bible and Slavery" (Ph.D. diss., Union Theological Seminary in the City of New York, 1995), 48. Of course, these meanings do not reside in the words themselves in abstraction. The point of the discussion is the meaning as an expression of industrial culture.

55. This is a slight adaptation and change from the list in Bruce C. Birch and Larry L. Rasmussen, *The Predicament of the Prosperous* (Philadelphia: Westminster Press, 1978), 44–45.

56. Frederic Morton, *Crosstown Sabbath: A Street Journey Through History* (New York: Grove Press, 1987), 31.

57. See the earlier discussion.

58. Hawken, 105–106.

59. Ibid., 106–107.

60. Ibid., 107, citing A. A. Berle and G. C. Means, *The Modern Corporation and Private Property* (New York: Macmillan Co., 1933).

61. "When Money Talks, Governments Listen," *New York Times*, 24 July 1994, sec. 4, p. 3.

62. Hawken, 197.

63. Ibid., 108.

64. H. Maurer, *Great Enterprise: Growth and Behavior of the Big Corporation* (New York: Macmillan, 1956), 167, quoted in Bas de Gaay Fortman, "Is Capitalism Possible?," State and Society Relations Paper, nos. 95–96 (The Hague, Netherlands: Institute of Social Studies, n.d.), 10.

65. Robert L. Heilbroner, Foreword to *The End of Work: The Decline of the Global Labor Force and the Dawn of the Post-Market Era*, by Jeremy Rifkin (New York: G. P. Putnam's Sons, 1995), xii; and Drucker, 54.

66. Drucker, 62.

67. Heilbroner in Rifkin, xii.

68. Ibid., xv.

69. Drucker, 55ff.

70. "U.S. Corporations Expanding Abroad at A Quicker Pace," *New York Times*, 25 July 1994, sec. A, p. 1. Those who think, however, that this means U.S. blue collar jobs have simply moved offshore, or that these industries will employ huge numbers of presently unemployed abroad, haven't been watching the technological trends and the establishment of jobless growth. The argument about exported jobs giving work to roughly parallel work populations elsewhere made some sense thirty years ago. It no longer captures the reality very well.

71. Marcos Terena, "Sing the Song of the Voice of the Forest," Chap. in *Story Earth: Native Voices on the Environment*, ed. Pablo Piacentini (San Francisco: Mercury House, 1993), 31–32.

72. Donna J. Haraway, *Simians, Cyborgs, and Women: The Reinvention of Nature* (New York: Routledge, 1991), 43, citing Frank Parsons, *Human Engineer* (n.p., 1894).

73. Haraway, *Simians, Cyborgs, and Women*, 164.

74. Drucker, 64.

75. Ibid.

76. Ibid., 74–75.

77. Ibid., 76.

78. Ibid., 78.

79. Gnosticism was a dualistic religious and philosophical movement of the late Hellenistic and early Christian periods in which promised salvation came through possession of a secret knowledge in the hands of an intellectual elite. In the Christian version, Jesus Christ, an intermediary sent by God, "descends" to earth in order to restore humankind, through saving knowledge, to its proper heavenly abode, its true home.

80. "Get on Line for Plato's Cave," *New York Times*, 25 June 1995, sec. E, p. 5.

81. The reference is to the popular Christian gnostic writing of the early Christian centuries, usually attributed to an influential gnostic, Valentius.

82. "At the Summit: New Leaders and Old, with New Agendas and Old," and "Group of 7 Summit Leaders Find There Is Little to Fix in Their Economies," *New York Times*, 8 July 1994, sec. A, p. 8.

83. See the discussion in "A Lingering Unease Despite Strong Growth," *New York Times*, 3 January 1995, sec. C, p. 1.

84. Fortman, 11.

85. David C. Korten, "Sustainable Development Strategies: The People-Centered Consensus" (n.p., The People-Centered Development Forum, 17 May 1994), 1.

86. Ibid.

87. Gustavo Esteva, "Basta!," *The Ecologist* 24, no. 3 (May/June 1994): 84–85.

88. Ibid., 84.

89. Ibid.

90. Ibid., 83–84.

91. Ibid., 83.

92. See the discussion of Korten, 6. I draw heavily from Korten's and Esteva's accounts.

93. Nicholas Hildyard, "Foxes in Charge of Chickens," Chap. in *Global Ecology*, ed. Wolfgang Sachs (London: Zed Books, 1993), 23.

94. Tariq Banuri, "The Landscape of Diplomatic Conflicts," Chap. in *Global Ecology*, 56–57.

95. This discussion of North/South is indebted to David C. Korten, "Sustainable Development," *World Policy Journal* (Winter 1991/92): 173–74.

96. We might add parenthetically that if the U.N. Earth Summit had winners, the North won. All the treaties protected access to resources for conventional sustainable development and none of them required less consumption and diminished standards of living in the North in order to address environmental constraints and poverty reduction. Ambassador Robert Ryan, head of the U.S. delegation, said at presummit meetings, as did President Bush, that the standard of living of U.S. citizens simply was "not up for negotiation" at the Earth Summit. And it wasn't. The South, and many Northerners with them, did succeed, however, in putting poverty reduction and environmental protection squarely on the global agenda *for everybody*. (These are written into the World Bank's mission statement, for example.) Yet prevailing economic relationships and dynamics were left in place, with the basic policy decisions of business and finance falling outside Rio's reach altogether. (This is the case with corporations and the World Bank as well, to continue the example.) Which is to say, Southern "victories" were written into the Northern pattern of ecoqualified development. See Maximo T. Kalaw, Jr., "The Response of the South to the Justice and Ecology Debate," in *Sustainable Growth—A Contradiction in Terms?* (Geneva: World Council of Churches, 1993), 54.

97. Korten, "Sustainable Development," 160–161.

98. Korten citing one of the conclusions of *Our Common Future*, in "Sustainable Development," 161.

99. Ibid.

100. Reported by Paul Ekins, "Making Development Sustainable," Chap. in *Global Ecology*, 92.

101. Truman as quoted by J. Ronald Engel, "Sustainable Development: A New Global Ethic?" *The Egg: An Eco-Justice Quarterly* 12, no. 1 (Winter 1991/92): 4.

102. Ibid., 5.

103. Ibid.

104. Wolfgang Sachs as cited by Wesley Granberg-Michaelson, *Redeeming the Creation, The Rio Summit: Challenge to the Churches* (Geneva: World Council of Churches, 1992), 1.

105. See the discussion in Ponting, *A Green History*, especially chap. 8, "Ways of Thought," 139–160.

106. Engel, 5.

107. Stephen Schmidheiny, "The Business Logic of Sustainable Development" *Columbia Journal of World Business* XXVII, nos. 3 & 4 (Fall/Winter 1992): 21. Schmidheiny's appeal to business is straightforward: "The bottom-line demand of the average business person is, 'Ethics and all that aside, give me one good business reason why I should care about the environment.' We [the Business Council] offer two. First, if you don't, your business will lose out in the coming environmental shake-out. Second, as the division between environmental excellence and economic excellence blurs, there will be increasing profitability and competitiveness in ecoefficiency" (22).

108. Korten, "Sustainable Development," 158–159.

109. William C. Clark, "Managing Planet Earth," *Scientific American* 261 (September 1989): 48.

110. Ibid., 47.

111. This listing of norms is a composite drawing from World Council of Churches' discussions as well as the Presbyterian Church (USA) draft of "Sustainable Development, Reformed Faith, and U.S. International Economic Policy."

112. Charles E. Curran, "Subsidiarity, Principle of," in *The Westminster Dictionary of Christian Ethics*, 1986. "Subsidiarity" is from the Latin *"subsidium,"* meaning "help."

113. A comment to the famous essay of Garrett Hardin, "The Tragedy of the Commons." Hardin's treatment is deceptive. Commons in preindustrial societies were generally well regulated by the communities to which they belonged and which depended on them. Hardin's portrayal of the destruction of the commons goes

like this. Each farmer discovers that it is in his or her self-interest to add a cow to his or her herd in the pasture (the commons) because he or she accrues all the economic benefits from the additional cow while sharing the costs (the common pasture). When many farmers act on this, the burden on the commons degrades it and may even destroy it as productive pasture. But this logic and practice is not that of the commons at all. It is free-standing individuals treating the commons, not as a commons, but an open-access system from which each might take as much as he or she can. A calculation of self-interest, with "nature" as essentially free goods and the market as the nexus, is the picture here. This is industrial system logic, not commons' logic. Commons' logic means community regulation of shared resources.

114. Stephen Viederman, "The Economics of Sustainability: Challenges," (Jessie Noyes Foundation, New York City), 17.

115. This example, including the citation from Jefferson, are taken from Ronald Heifetz, *Leadership Without Easy Answers* (Cambridge, MA: The Belknap Press of Harvard University Press, 1994), 88–100. Readers may wish to see my chapter, "Shaping Community," which also uses this example, in a volume on essential practices for the twenty-first century as these are instructed by Jewish and Christian traditions. See Dorothy Bass and Craig Dykstra, eds., *Practicing Our Faith: A Way of Life for a Searching People* (San Francisco: Jossey-Bass, 1997).

116. Hawken, 190.

117. David Wann, *Deep Design: Pathways to a Livable Future* (Washington, D.C.: Island Press, 1996), 196–197.

118. Hawken, 166.

119. Wann, 197.

120. Cited by Wann, 140.

121. Ibid.

122. See Aaron Sachs, *Eco-Justice: Linking Human Rights and the Environment* (Washington, D.C.: The Worldwatch Institute, 1995), 31–33.

123. Ibid., 32.

124. Ibid., 50.

125. The examples from Japan and Germany are included among others in Wann, *Deep Design*, 43–46.

126. Wann, 166–167.

127. Ibid., 172–173.

128. Elizabeth Hanson, Review of *The Rarest of the Rare*, by Diane Ackerman, *New York Times Book Review*, 18 February 1996, p. 11.

129. This is the summary of design principles from Sim van der Ryn and Stuart Cowan, *Ecological Design* (Washington, DC and Covelho, CA: Island Press, 1996), 54–56. The rest of the book is an elaboration of these, with multiple examples.

130. The principles are from David W. Orr, *Ecological Literacy: Education and the Transition to a Post-modern World* (Albany: State University of New York Press, 1992), 29–30.

Bibliography

Banuri, Tariq. "The Landscape of Diplomatic Conflicts." In *Global Ecology*. London: Zed Books, 1993.

Barney, Gerald O., Jane Blewett, and Kristen R. Barney. *Global 2000 Revisited: What Shall We Do?* Arlington, Va: Public Interest Publications, 1993.

Bass, Dorothy, and Craig Dykstra, eds. *Practicing Our Faith: A Way of Life for a Searching People*. San Francisco: Jossey-Bass Publishers, 1996.

Ben-David, Shemaya. *Megiddo Armageddon*. N.p., 1979.

Berry, Wendell. "Does Community Have a Value?" In *Home Economics*. San Francisco: North Point Press, 1987.

Birch, Bruce C., and Larry L. Rasmussen. *The Predicament of the Prosperous*. Philadelphia: Westminster Press, 1978.

Clark, William C. "Managing Planet Earth." *Scientific American* 261 (September 1989).

Crosby, Alfred W. *Ecological Imperialism: The Biological Expansion of Europe, 900–1900*. Cambridge: Cambridge University Press, 1986.

Drucker, Peter. "The Age of Social Transformation." *The Atlantic Monthly*, November 1994.

Engel, J. Ronald. "Sustainable Development: A New Global Ethic?" *The Egg: An Eco-Justice Quarterly* 12, no. 1 (Winter 1991–92).

Esteva, Gustavo. "Basta!" *The Ecologist* 24, no. 3 (May/June 1994).

Fortman, Bas de Gaay. "Is Capitalism Possible?" State and Society Relations Paper nos. 95–96. The Hague, Netherlands: Institute of Social Studies, n.d.

Granberg-Michaelson, Wesley. *Redeeming the Creation, The Rio Earth Summit: Challenge to the Churches.* Geneva: World Council of Churches Publication, 1992.

Haraway, Donna. *Primate Visions: Gender, Race and Nature in the World of Modern Science.* New York: Routledge, 1989.

———. *Simians, Cyborgs, and Women: The Reinvention of Nature.* New York: Routledge, 1991.

Hawken, Paul. *The Ecology of Commerce.* New York: Harper Business, 1993.

Heifetz, Ronald. *Leadership Without Easy Answers.* Cambridge, Mass.: The Belknap Press of Harvard University Press, 1994.

Heilbroner, Robert L. Foreword to *The End of Work: The Decline of the Global Labor Force and the Dawn of the Post-Market Era,* by Jeremy Rifkin. New York: G. Putnam's Sons, 1995.

Hildyard, Nicholas. "Foxes in Charge of Chickens." In *Global Economy,* ed. Wolfgang Sachs, London: Zed Books, 1993.

Hutchison, G. Whit. "The Bible and Slavery." Ph.D. diss., Union Theological Seminary in the City of New York, 1995.

Kalaw, Jr., Maximo T. "The Response of the South to the Justice and Ecology Debate." In *Sustainable Growth—A Contradiction in Terms?* Geneva: World Council of Churches, 1993.

Korten, David C. "Sustainable Development Strategies: The People-Centered Consensus." The People-Centered Development Forum, 17 May 1994.

———. "Sustainable Development." *World Policy Journal* (Winter 1991–92).

Maguire, Daniel. *The Moral Core of Judaism and Christianity: Reclaiming the Revolution.* Minneapolis: Fortress Press, 1993.

McNeill, William H. *The Human Condition: An Ecological and Historical View.* Princeton, NJ: Princeton University Press, 1980.

——— . *Plagues and Peoples.* Garden City, NY: Anchor Doubleday, 1976.

Mies, Maria, and Vandana Shiva. *Ecofeminism.* London: Zed Books, 1993.

Morton, Frederic. *Crosstown Sabbath: A Street Journey through History.* New York: Grove Press, 1987.

National Round Table on the Environment and the Economy. "The Challenge." *1991–92 Annual Review.* Ottawa: National Round Table Secretariat, 1992.

Orr, David W. *Ecological Literacy: Education and the Transition to a Post-Modern World.* Albany, N.Y.: State University of New York Press, 1992.

Ponting, Clive. *A Green History of the World: The Environment and the Collapse of Great Civilizations.* New York: Penguin Books, 1991.

Sachs, Aaron. *Eco-Justice: Linking Human Rights and the Environment.* Washington, D.C.: The Worldwatch Institute, 1995.

Sachs, Wolfgang, ed. *Global Ecology.* London: Zed Books, 1993.

Schmidheiny, Stephen. "The Business Logic of Sustainable Development." *Columbia Journal of World Business* XXVII (Fall/Winter 1992).

Swimme, Brian, and Thomas Berry. *The Universe Story.* San Francisco: Harper San Francisco, 1992.

Terena, Marcos. "Sing the Song of the Voice of the Forest." In *Story Earth: Native Voices on the Environment.* San Francisco: Mercury House, 1993.

van der Ryn, Sim, and Stuart Cowan. *Ecological Design.* Washington, D.C. and Covelho, Calif.: Island Press, 1996.

Viederman, Stephen. "The Economics of Sustainability: Challenges." Jessie Noyes Foundation, New York City, n.d.

Wann, David. *Deep Design: Pathways to a Livable Future.* Washington, D.C.: Island Press, 1996.

Weiskel, Timothy C. "In Dust and Ashes: The Environmental Crisis in Religious Perspective." *Harvard Divinity Bulletin* 21, no. 3 (1992).

Index